Thoughts

on

Leadership

Second Edition

... A 'MUST READ'

For All New

Managers &

Leaders

John P. McWilliams

Thoughts On Leadership

Copyright 2016
By John P. McWilliams

First printing: August 2016
Second printing: October 2017

Reservation of Rights

All rights reserved. No part of this publication may be reproduced or transmitted in any form or by any means, electronic or mechanical, including photocopying, recording, or any information storage and retrieval system, without the express written permission from the author and/or the publisher.

ISBN-13: 978-1537065892 (CreateSpace-Assigned)
ISBN-10: 1537065890

Published by Amazon Create Space

Tel.: (866) 356-2153
Website: www.createspace.com

Printed in the United States of America

Disclaimer

The Publisher, CreateSpace (Amazon), and the author hereby exclude all liability to the extent permitted by the law for any errors or omissions, or opinions expressed in this book and for any loss, damage or expense (whether direct or indirect) suffered by a third party relying on any information contained in the text or within illustrations, or photographs contained in this book.

Dedication

I dedicate this book to all Leaders of every kind for the great work they do!

"Great leaders lead through example
and then others desire to follow."

- John P. McWilliams

Other Works[1,2] By The Same Author

Non-Fiction

New Mexico: A Glimpse Into An Enchanted Land
(Out of Print - send an email to author at:
2braveharts@gmail.com)

Against the Wind: Courageous Apache Women[1,2]

Poetry/Poetic Memoir

Days of Innocence (Poetic Memoir)[1]

Ramblings (Poetry)[1]

Short Stories- Fiction

Santa's Favorite Christmas Tales[1]

[1] See www.amazon.com for purchase
[2] See www.barnesandnoble.com for purchase

Table of Contents

Acknowledgements ix
Preface xi

INTRODUCTION 1

PART ONE: CHARACTERISTICS OF A 'GOOD, EFFECTIVE' LEADER 7
Leadership 9
Leadership Deja Vu 13
What You Know And What You Don't Know 17
Micro-Management: A 'No-No' 19
Setting Priorities For All Activities 23
Approachability & Availability 27
Clear Communications 29
Customer Relations 33
Projected Self-Assurance and Confidence: Leadership Essentials 37
Decisiveness in Leadership 39
Honesty & Integrity: Necessary Characteristics of an Effective Leader 45
Posture and Leadership 49

Table of Contents - Continued

How You Show Your Hands..53
Murphy's Law and What You See Is What You Get 57
Credibility..59
Necessary Essentials: Mutual Respect and Genuine Humility..63
Being Bold & Persistent..67
The Significance of Effective Experience..............................71
Pettiness and Self-Defensiveness: Incompatible With Leadership...75
Smile: Friendliness Goes a Long Way..................................79
Recognizing Performance...83
Delegation & Empowerment...85
Unity, Not Divisiveness...87

PART TWO: SPECIFIC TECHNIQUES FOR LEADERS..89
The Importance of Planning...91
Organizing For Success...95
Team Building: Another Element in Success.....................99
Team Building Continued: The 'Special' Sauce...............103
Management By Walking Around (MBWA).....................107
Running Short But Effective Meetings.............................111
E-Mail Saturation And How To Survivie It......................117
Stress Management..121

APPENDICES..*125*
Appendix A: Work Breakdown Structures (WBS)............127

Table of Contents - Continued

Appendix B: Earned Value Systems (EVM) For Large Projects..133
Appendix C: Key Contract Types.....................................139
Appendix D: General Discussion......................................145

About the Author..151

Thoughts On Leadership

Acknowledgments

I wish to acknowledge all my many mentors across a space of 38 years for their guidance their shared experience and their wisdom! I'd never have learned about leadership and management but for their wonderful direction. Thanks also for all the gray hairs, in later years, due to many 'scary' assignments. I earned from every one of them. One truly learns from one's own mistakes and from the mistakes of others. Seldom do we learn, as effectively, from our hard-earned successes.

The Author

Thoughts On Leadership

Preface

The title, *Thoughts on Leadership*, refers to thoughts that have imposed themselves on me, especially after my early Retirement, when I had more time to review and to think on past experiences. These thoughts pertain, of course, to management and leadership.

The emphasis in this small book is pragmatic: readability, informability, enjoyability and comprehension. My hope is that many of the lessons and insights gained over my 38-year career can be and will be passed along to a new and budding breed of managers and leaders.

The majority of thoughts contained herein, came about from a closer examination of past assignments and management/leadership experiences. Some assignments allowed me to manage and lead a program team from start to finish, from proposal to contract completion, while other assignments were to rescue failing projects and bring them to a successful conclusion. Many times this was a very big order. Nonetheless, I applied many of the principles described in this book and success was often the end result. I sincerely wish the reader happy and informative reading as one proceeds through this book.

One theme that is repeated numerous times, intentionally, throughout this book is the need to project positivity and assurance, so that other team members may feel assured that success under such a 'leader' is a real possibility. How one projects this image can take many forms, as described in this book, but the end effect is unchanged: confidence in the 'leader' by following his or her 'lead'.

Thoughts On Leadership

This book is organized into two main parts followed by four Appendices. Part One describes many, but not all, of the main characteristics I have found in good and effective leaders and managers. Part Two describes some of the tools used by project managers to bring about assignment success. The following Appendices provide an overview of some specific tools used by technical development project managers, and so may not be applicable to more general leadership discussions. That is why they are included here in the Appendices. Non-technical leaders may wish to skip these Appendices for that reason.

Appendix A briefly addresses Work Breakdown Structures (WBS) to organize and collect task costs in a methodical manner; Appendix B discusses Earned Value Measurement Systems (EVMS), which is very useful in gauging a project's true accomplishments, instead of just the schedule and cost to achieve such progress. Appendix C details various popular and common contract types. This summary is by no means complete or exhaustive. Appendix D provides a closing discussion of leadership once again.

A brief biography of the author is then presented.

I truly hope that some new leaders will find this information useful and effective in ensuring the success of their own assignments. Please enjoy!!

The Author

Introduction

I have thought, why write yet another book on 'leadership'? There are already numerous books available on various aspects of this intriguing topic. What could I possibly add?

After some examination, and after reviewing numerous blogs that I had written on the once-operational Apache Management website, I have decided that I did indeed have much to say. For one thing, this book emphasizes the characteristics required of an effective 'leader'.

A project or program manager, or a store manager is exactly that: a 'leader'. He or she leads a team towards achievement of the project or sales goals by various means certainly, but mainly by means of personality. That is the key lesson that I have learned through a long, successful career. This is not to undermine the importance of control, but in the end the 'control' is once again over the actions and behavior of 'human beings'. These rules apply to all people in all situations and therefore are generally applicable, in various, seemingly unrelated areas.

Gender also has little to do with it. When I became a Director of MSD Programs, I hired a number of females, with extraordinary talents to manage several projects. I found them to be highly effective, sometimes more effective than male project managers...although I had some very good ones there too.

However, I found that the most successful leaders maintained many of the qualities mentioned within this short book. These technical managers knew of course, about EVM,

WBS's, and the differences among various contract types, and much more. In other words, they knew the technical aspects of project management, but they also possessed many of the personal behavioral qualities that are discussed herein.

I have since encountered Retail Sales managers/leaders. Although many of the job specifics are different, the principles of good leadership still apply, because there exists a motivational need that must be communicated to other human beings, whose needs and wants are very similar to those of other humans in other fields. Hence, many of the principles of leadership discussed in this book also apply to almost any field of endeavor that includes leading teams of human beings.

I have seen that many of these same leadership characteristics apply in non-technical fields. I found this to be true in my own experience, when I was a working first as a technical project manager and director, and second as a sales clerk in a large mercantile store.

The problem or the issue in writing a book of this type is in defining what NOT to include. The responsibilities and the skills required to be an effective leader, of any kind, are vast and wide. There are so many topics, so many skills required that the list is truly daunting. Effective experience is still the best teacher however. To be truthful, some have a natural ability that experience can enhance and amplify, while some don't and never will become effective leaders, because they possess an impediment of some sort to learning. It may be personality, stubbornness, age, small-mindedness, lack of ambition, or some other form of resistance.

In the middle of my career I came across several young senior engineers who desired to become project managers. They enrolled to receive Master's Degrees in

Introduction

Project Management (PM) or to get certified in this field. So they were assigned as PM's for some difficult development projects. This is discussed later in one of the chapters in Part One. To make the story short, since it is more fully explained elsewhere, they failed miserably. Why? Because of an insufficiency of practical effective experience. It became a matter of book learning vs practical experience. The lack of the latter caused them to fail, in spite of their advanced PM degrees.

They lacked the proper personality characteristics that are defined to some extent in Part One of this book. Not only did they lack the required personality, they lacked the respect of their reports. Why? Inexperience. They were not respected because of their immaturity and their lack of relevant experience. They simply were not ready, even if their own department managers thought differently.

Anyone can become a project manager or program manager, but very few can become 'effective' leaders, without the right personality, knowledge of the technical aspects of their area of responsibility, and sufficient relevant and successful prior experience.

Without sufficient relevant and successful experience, the 'wool' can easily be pulled over the eyes of the inexperienced. I have witnessed this first hand. Without sufficient experience, there is no credibility, which is essential to any leader. Once credibility is gone, respect soon follows and then disaster strikes.

Although Retail Sales and other businesses have a different specific emphasis, the key characteristics of a great leader are the same, and common among them. There may be a difference in the type of specific knowledge needed in each position but the ability to 'lead' is either natural or learned by sometimes 'bitter' experience. These same leaders, in different fields, often demonstrate the same characteristics outlined in Part One of this book.

I have another anecdote to summarize here to prove my point. Once, while reviewing a very large contract a very effective experienced PM, who clearly 'knew his stuff', tried to pull the proverbial wool over my eyes. Only, it did not work because I had had enough experience of my own to recognize the situation. I mentioned this and the attempt failed. I told him so, and he never again tried to 'fool' me. What was the crucial difference here?...effective experience.

He had been caught! How does one do that without sufficient effective experience? The straight-forward answer is it cannot be done. That is why I say in one of the discussions that, given the choice, I would rather take (effective) 'experience' any time over 'inexperience'.

However, more than experience is required to be an 'effective' leader.

A leader needs to be approachable, bold, decisive, organized, show confidence while also showing mutual respect for others, possess a sense of honesty and integrity, have team-building capabilities, be comfortable with planning and constant re-planning, demonstrate good posture, be capable of understanding customer needs, be an excellent communicator (both written and oral), be disciplined and be a true 'leader' of others. These characteristics apply to any and all leaders in any specific field, not just to leaders in technical development management.

Finding all these myriad qualities in one person can be difficult but not impossible. Some people excel at these naturally, others do not. Those who excel, with adequate relevant and effective experience can often make excellent and effective leaders. Not many 'leaders' possess all these skills or personality traits, but a selected few do. However,

Introduction

many of these skills can be learned and that is the purpose of this book.

This book is in no way exhaustive. It is not meant to be. Many books have been written about the very topics I have and have not discussed here. Many of the topics discussed in this book have been discussed in many of the blogs that I have written in the Apache Management website (www.apachemgmtconsult.com). I have rewritten or edited some of these as chapters in this book, while other chapters have been written specifically for this short treatise. These are the ramblings of a once 'effective' PM and leader.

As mentioned earlier, I have gained some additional experience and exposure in the Retail space since I left engineering development. I have, since my Retirement, found many similarities between the leaders and effective managers in the Retail Sales space, and 'great' leaders in the technical development fields. This has bolstered my intrinsic belief that 'leadership' principles and characteristics apply everywhere. It is easily recognized that what IS different is the specific knowledge required in each field. This too can be obtained by application and relevant experience, but the basics of great 'leadership' remain unchanged and generally applicable. This observation has motivated me to write this book.

I am enjoying my Retirement now. I have written about non-management topics (see www. briaventures.com). I have enjoyed my career, but now it is time to hand over the baton to the next generation of leaders. My hope is that this short book will help many young aspiring professionals to embrace leadership, in any form. It is difficult, yes, but it can also be extremely rewarding and satisfying. I genuinely hope that others will read these discussions and find that they have 'what it takes', that they have the 'right stuff', as they say, to become effective leaders.

    My intention here is to pass on to another generation what I have spent an entire career learning. Hopefully, it will be of some value to those who wish to learn 'leadership' skills from an experienced leader/manager.

-The Author

Part One:

Characteristics

of a

'Good, Effective'

Leader

Thoughts On Leadership

Part 1: Characteristics of a Good, Effective Leader

Leadership

We all know what 'leadership' is when we see it or experience it. Yet, defining it is a bit more difficult. I will do my best to get a handle on what 'leadership' is.

From my own experience, I see leadership as a multi-pronged set of characteristics. To reduce this to its simplest definition, I would say that leadership is the ability to enlist others in the successful execution of the leader's stated vision. It requires a 'breaking of the mold', as they say. In other words, a leader is someone who goes beyond the 'status quo' and reaches out with the voluntary support of others, who are willing to follow and execute the leader's stated vision. A good leader is never a follower.

There is also some confusion about what differentiates a leader and a manager. It is possible for a single individual to wear 'both hats'. Generally speaking, a leader seeks to be successful in the execution of his own vision, while a manager seeks to be successful too, but most often it is some other person's vision that is being executed. Nonetheless, both roles can be assumed at the same time and in the same person, and often are.

Leadership requires certain characteristics. An effective leader is confident and exudes that confidence to others. Leadership also requires decisiveness and trust. These last two items usually come about from the adequate effective experience of the leader. "It is better to make a timely 'bad' decision than an untimely decision of any kind."

Hesitation can be corrosive, as it can eat away at the team's confidence in the leader. However, the 'leader' must also be competent in his or her decision-making. Without allegiance, mutual respect and trust, and a clearly stated vision by the leader, as well as the other qualities mentioned above, there can be no true effective or successful leadership.

'Good judgement' in decision making is also important. Such judgement usually, but not always, comes about from sufficient 'effective' experience. A 'leader' will become recognized for his or her 'good judgement'. If the individual becomes known instead for constantly and consistently exercising 'poor judgement' that also will become known and the opportunity to function as an effective leader will likewise diminish.

Respect and trust must be mutual. Else, there will only remain a destructive mistrust, which can only act counter to the successful execution and fulfillment of the leader's stated vision. Of course, the success of any leader's mission requires competent, capable, self-driven and motivated staff. Hence, proper team staffing and team building are essential qualities or abilities of an effective leader.

Realistic planning is essential, but such planning should be seen only as an ever-changing roadmap to the successful execution of the leader's vision. The plan must be dynamic, meaning it should be updated as new challenges and possible opportunities unfold with time. I have seen many project managers make the common mistake of either never updating their plan, or only updating it when a project is already overrun cost-wise, delayed schedule-wise or somehow not meeting the projected performance requirements (techical, sales, etc). A plan should never be a static document. It should be dynamic and ever-changing to reflect reality and any recent changes from initial assumptions. Think of a plan as a tool. If the tool doesn't work, get another, or a better one. The leader and the plan need to be flexible and adaptive. Either too much optimism

Part 1: Characteristics of a Good, Effective Leader

(unrealistic) or too much pessimism (too negative) will undermine a team's confidence in its leader. Realism is generally respected most. Also, it is important for the leader to have one or more 'back-up plans' in the event that previous assumptions do not unfold as predicted.

This is what defines the major difference between a gambler and an effective leader. Both can take great risks. But the 'leader' has 'back-up' plans to implement in the event that the worst case materializes. Generally, the gambler's only plan is to minimize losses, or to leave. Seizing unexpected opportunities is also important and may require some measure of replanning. (Back-up plans can be modified to exploit new, unforeseen opportunities.)

Projecting positive body language is a quality possessed by many effective leaders. Most prospective leaders probably do this intuitively. Others can learn many of these techniques to eventually become effective and efficient leaders.

Effective performance and mutual respect are the only measures by which a 'leader' gains respect. Title alone has no bearing, in most cases. While a title may grant authority, it cannot, by itself, garner respect. An effective leader must earn respect, the 'hard' way. That is, respect must be 'earned'. Leadership is attainable by anyone willing to implement many of the characteristics mentioned in this book.

The last thing I want to talk about is the concept of 'leadership from behind.' Anyone who has had any experience leading military teams, project teams., sales teams or something similar, knows from that experience that such a concept is an oxymoron. Teams respond to 'out front' leadership and guidance. This has been so for thousands of years. 'Leadership from behind' means only one thing. It leaves a leadership vacuum that will be filled by a different 'real' leader. It only means that the self-appointed leader 'will be left behind'. Further, he or she who espouses "leadership from behind' will eventually find himself or herself there in the back alone, while others follow another 'out front' leader, who is willing to share risks similar to their own.

'Leadership from behind' appears cowardly and lacking in 'good judgement' to the rank and file, because it does not appear to be real 'leadership'. If not that, then such behaviour shows a lack of commitment or a real uncertainty... anathema to anyone aspiring to true 'leadership'.

The term 'charisma' is often thrown around as a characteristic possessed by a 'leader'. However, 'charisma' is merely the embodiment of most of the characteristics described in this book.

Part 1: Characteristics of a Good, Effective Leader

Leadership Déjà Vu

In the last discussion, entitled 'Leadership', I stated some of my observations based upon my many years of practical and pragmatic successful management experience. That experience includes task management, line management. project management, systems engineering and a divisional directorship over all projects run by MSD (Multi-channel Systems Division), the largest and most profitable division in the last company for which I worked.

However, just recently I heard, in the Primaries, some candidates for POTUS express their own definitions of what this intangible we call 'leadership' is exactly. One candidate stated that 'leadership' is about breaking the status quo. Another said that 'leadership' is not about what one says one will do but what one has actually done. Leadership does indeed require both of these elements in the 'leader's' make-up and background. However, I still believe that these are 'necessary but not sufficient' for an aspirant to become an effective leader.

An effective leader must be able to coalesce others through mutual trust and confidence so that they will work endlessly to achieve the leader's goals and hence the over-arching project or corporate goals. In so doing, the leader's goals become, quite naturally, the team's goals. The characteristics described by the political candidates, as stated above, are certainly helpful. While I think on it, there is one more characteristic that helps a leader.

That is approachability. A leader should always be open and approachable by his staff. This means that the leader should be available to his or her staff, most of the time. 'Lack of accessibility' or 'approachability' means that the staff cannot get in touch with the leader because of several reasons: physical unavailability, intimidation by the leader, no other mean of communication is provided, the leader seems to be too busy, etc.

None of these are acceptable. A leader must always be accessible because it helps build 'team spirit' and it is necessary for timely conmmunication by the staff of issues and problems that may need immediate attention.

In addition, the leader should never be afraid to make a mistake, or even to admit to one. Leaders who so expose themselves, or put themselves at risk are usually greatly respected for their self-assurance. If one doesn't know the answer, do not be afraid to say so. It only shows one's 'humanness', and more easily allows the staff to see the leader as 'approachable' and 'reasonable'. However, a leader must use this 'honesty' sparingly, in order to maintain the 'higher ground' at all times. Respect is ephemeral.

But one must ask the obvious question. How does one explain the following? Some selected individuals become distinctive 'leaders' without the need for very much in the way of previous skill or experience. They seem to be 'fast-learners' or 'they know instinctively.' If only everyone was so blessed or fortunate. The good news is that for the rest of us, many of the necessary skills for effective leadership can be learned!

That is not to say that experience is not important. It is VERY important. It teaches one how to make difficult decisions. It teaches one how to make multiple decisions often with a dire shortage of complete (100%) information or understanding. The answer lies in the fact that (effective) 'experience' or 'what one has done already' (successfully)

Part 1: Characteristics of a Good, Effective Leader

is indeed 'necessary but by itself, it is 'insufficient'. Such (effective) 'experience' gives others a sense that the possessor of that experience is perhaps properly equipped with the right mental, emotional, political, project and people skills that enable the individual to make wise decisions.

The 'sufficient' category is completed by the implementation of other characteristics that have already been identified previously. In summary, the leader must fulfill the definition as given above. If he or she is incapable of using integrity, honesty, team building, organizational abilities, mutual respect and timely decision-making, to enlist others to execute the stated goal(s), then he or she will have great difficulty in ever becoming an 'effective and successful' leader. If, on the other hand, one can do what we have talked about above on a regular basis, one can 'learn' to become an effective 'leader'.

Thoughts On Leadership

Part 1: Characteristics of a Good, Effective Leader

What You Know and What you Don't Know

Any effective 'leader' is aware of his or her own capabilities. However, it is just as important, perhaps more so, to admit what one lacks, to be aware of one's own limitations. We are all human after all. None of us are perfect, no matter how much we may think we know. The key is to recognize our individual shortcomings, but also to take the appropriate action to correct the deficiency. Paramount are confidence and self-assurance, without cockiness. There is a certain genuine 'humility' required here, borne by experience and competence that radiates from an 'effective' leader.

This requires discipline and a certain amount of modesty. It means admitting to others, as well as oneself, what is lacking in the team, which does include the leader, in this case. Surround oneself with those who are knowledgeable in the areas that the leader lacks. This demonstrates, in no uncertain way, that the 'leader' is confident enough and self-assured enough to admit his own deficiency and to fulfill that need with someone who has the appropriate and relevant experience. This is a true sign of 'leadership'.

There are cases where the 'leader' is not 'big enough' to acknowledge such a deficiency. This is usually the case, with an individual who lacks the self-confidence that comes with sufficient experience. In such a case, the individual feels a 'need' to prove to others that he or she is capable. This can give rise to an inflated sense of self-importance and an inclination to ignore the advice of other well-meaning individuals, even when these same individuals might present reasonable solutions to the problem at hand. Such 'smallness of mind' has no place in a leader. Further, it will be noticed by the rest of the team to the detriment of the leader. Failure to recognize one's own shortcomings, and we all have them, can be perceived as 'arrogance', or 'bullheadedness', that is usually self-blinding and often erroneous.

I have also seen cases where those with limited self-confidence or very isolated, specialized knowledge hold onto that knowledge and protect it jealously, because they realize deep down inside that 'knowledge is power' and so they never wish to reveal the source of their knowledge or the knowledge itself to others, for fear of losing their own influence.

These behaviours are certainly not a formula for 'success' as a leader. Other more experienced individuals can quickly see through the charade. They are self-limiting and make failure almost inevitable. What is not understood is that a truly 'effective' leader does not have to know everything. In fact, it is denying reality. Each of us is mortal and human, and prone to mistakes, errors and insufficiencies, which we must recognize, admit and correct, as necessary. The morale: try not to be a 'know it all'. It is self-defeating.

What is also important is to be decisive and bold. This is discussed elsewhere. Humble oneself. In the end, one will be respected for the self-recognition and for the self-acknowledgement that there is a need to be filled. Further, once the need is filled, the hiring is usually sanctioned by the needing 'leader'. The 'leader' will then automatically receive the loyalty of the newly assigned individual who is chosen or hired to fill the deficiency.

No one will think less of the leader for admitting to others that there is a team deficiency that needs to be filled, or that the 'leader' does not possess the needed capability.

Part 1: Characteristics of a Good, Effective Leader

Instead, there will be admiration for the 'leader' being astute and self-humbling enough to recognize the need, and who takes positive action to correct the 'insufficiency', by any means necessary.

Thoughts On Leadership

Part 1: Characteristics of a Good, Effective Leader

Micro-Management: A 'No-No'

What is micro-management? It is the tendency for a 'leader' to believe that he or she knows best about 'everything'. It leads to a belief that he or she knows better than the staff how to do a given task. Such a leader is perceived as a 'know it all'. Very undesirable.

Such a micro-manager then subsequently interferes or somehow hijacks the activity, such that the person assigned to the task feels undermined and 'unworthy'. This can lead to serious animosity on the part of the individual being undermined. Not only that, the entire team sees this and it negatively affects team morale.

As a general rule micro-management is very undesirable. It negatively affects the morale of the team, as each team member wonders who will be next. It demonstrates a 'lack of confidence or faith' by the leader that the assigned person is capable of performing the task. If there truly exists such a lack of confidence in the assigned person, then perhaps a better approach is to replace that incompetent person, long before the team morale plummets.

Micro-management itself, is usually justifiably frowned upon. Therefore, it ought to be avoided. This is often difficult to do, when the 'micro-manager' is under stress to 'perform or produce'. It takes years of experience to 'trust' in the ability of others, especially when one knows that one can do the same thing oneself, perhap even better. However, one must resist this great temptation, while one is responsible for the results of others. One has to train oneself to stand aside, and await the desired result. It is difficult but it can be done. As a leader, one needs to get out of the way. It is the only way that the assignee will learn and eventually 'grow' in experience. Let the assignee 'sink or swim' on his or her own merits. Advice is okay but interference is not!

Do not become codependent or an enabler, by running to one's assistance every time there is a 'problem'. Let the assignee figure it out. Advise that person to seek help from other more knowledgeable team members, so that the individual 'learns' that the effort is truly a 'team effort'.

However, for every rule there is an exception and this is no different. There are situations where a lesser degree of micro-management may become necessary. For example, sometimes there is no way to hire or transfer someone to complete a necessary task, especially tasks of very short duration. Yet the task may be essential. Should the skill to do the task be a capability of the 'leader', there are situations where the 'leader' may take on the responsibility, provided that the overall management of the project does not suffer and provided that the 'help' is merely temporary and transient. This is very important. Wherever possible, do not interfere, and do not micro-manage, unless by very rare exception, as the following example illustrates.

Once I found myself, as a project manager in just such a situation. I really did not want to get involved, but there was a very short-term need on the project to provide some impedance transformations. No one but I knew how to do this. I had learned this in my previous experience in Receiver Design with my first employer. It was a small duration, well-contained task. I was torn. I did not wish to get involved or to interfere but after careful consideration, I decided that the program needed my help...but for a very short duration only. I decided that I'd assist the junior engineer quickly and then get out of the way.

Part 1: Characteristics of a Good, Effective Leader

Hiring or transferring someone else to do this short task was unfeasible. Hence, I showed a more junior engineer how to do it. He learned from the process and my involvement only lasted less than a week. The junior engineer did not feel threatened. On the contrary, he was grateful for the assistance.

One other case applies, but again by exception only. In this other case, the task again was of short duration. The subtask was however on the Critical Path of the project. Therefore it was crucial to complete it in a timely manner, and the task was showing some difficulty in achieving its goal. In that particular case, the task was still done by another assigned person, but it required much more scrutiny and monitoring than usual. Successful task completion was necessary in order for the project to succeed. Once the task was completed, project scrutiny and monitoring returned to its normal level.

In summary, there are very few cases where micromanagement is justified, but as with every rule there are minor and rare exceptions. What must be born in mind is that, should it ever become necessary, the interruption is brief and short in time. Then get out of the way. As a leader, you generally don't belong there. Prolonged involvement at that level can also diminish the team's view of the leader, and bring him or her down in their view. Not good!

Thoughts On Leadership

Part 1: Characteristics of a Good, Effective Leader

__Setting Priorities for All Activities__

      Have you ever noticed that there never seems to be enough time to do all that is required of you? Meetings with staff/customers/bosses, mail of all kinds (e-mail, phone mail, physical mail), status reports to staff/management/customers, generation of meeting minutes, documentation, reviews, managing the staff and oversight of the overall project or effort, etc. The list seems almost endless. There are only so many hours in a day, even when one contributes one's own time. It seems impossible to do.

      Yet there is a way to manage it all. Time-wasters need not apply! The key is to establish priorities for every effort. Some subtasks need to be more timely or they are more pressing than others. For example, a leader can't really say 'No' when the CEO or the customer asks to be briefed or if there is a regularly scheduled status/review meeting with the Executive staff. There are also sub-tasks that are more important than others. There are tasks that lie on the Critical Path (CP) of a development project or that simply must be completed before other tasks can begin. These are most important because they determine the overall schedule. They are tied 1:1 with regard to overall performance. In other words, a one week slip in a CP task or some other critical task usually results in a one week slip in the total overall schedule. There are other tasks that may depend on another task's completion. Meanwhile staff may be standing idle, burning up costs with zero productivity, waiting for the task to complete because the output of that task is necessary for the following task.

Alternately, the leader may find that an effort is extremely fast-paced and that a list of several hundred Action Items (AI's) must be completed over a span of time and reviewed daily. These Action Items may require to have priorities established in order to allow an orderly and timely assignment of resources. Some AI's may be more crucial than others. One can identify many, many examples, but the main point is that not enough can possibly be accomplished unless all limiting factors are considered and appropriate priorities are set.

This holds true in daily life too. Usually, one cannot achieve everything in a single day. Hence, one must prioritize that which is absolutely necessary to achieve, and that which can wait some time. Some activities can stop the world if they are not achieved in a timely manner. Others do not have such an important effect. Only by prioritizing can one prevent the world from collapsing while other tasks get delayed but with little consequence.

Consequence is the primary determinant in setting priorities. What happens should I not be able to complete that activity today, or now? That is the driving force behind establishing any priority to anything.

Learn to keep a running list of Things To Do Today. That sometimes helps, but again it all comes down to setting priorities in the first place. Such a list without assigned prioities is useless.

If the list of Things To Do keeps growing as the day progresses, review the priorities accordingly. As items get accomplished and closed out there is a growing sense of achievement, and a diminished sense of being overwhelmed. Again, organization and prioritization conquers all.

Setting priorities is a way of organizing your activities

Part 1: Characteristics of a Good, Effective Leader

in an ordered way so that the most important or most timely are done first, and the lessor priorities are done at some later time, or maybe not at all. Reviewing and re-reviewing the established priorities is also very important, especially as new events occur. These new events may change the need to get certain tasks done according to the old or existing priority list. Hence, review and re-assignment of priorities may became necessary as the day or week progresses.

Never be afraid to re-assign priorities. It is 'par for the course'. In addition, always remember that, 'the only constant is change itself'. It is a concept that many are uncomfortable with, but it is true nonetheless. Plan for it but hope it will never occur.

Thoughts On Leadership

Part 1: Characteristics of a Good, Effective Leader

Approachability & Availability

A leader must always be approachable and available to his or her staff. This has been briefly alluded to before. We will expand on this simple concept here. Situations arise that may need the leader's immediate attention. Further, the staff needs to feel that the leader is not aloof or distant. Aloofness or a lack of either approachability or reasonable availability, is usually perceived as not allowing adequate communication or even direction, when it is needed most. It may be interpreted as either uncaring, or unimportant to the leader.

A leader's door should alway be open except in rare cases where the leader must close the door in order to complete his or her own work, or to find time to unwind from what is often overwhelming stress. Likewise if that 'door open' option is unavailable then the staff person should be able to commmunicate his or her concerns or need for direction by some other means, such as telephone or e-mail.

A staff member should never be made to feel that his or her concerns are either unimportant or unworthy of the leader's consideration.

An open door speaks volumes about someone's availablility. Nor should a staff person ever feel intimidated about the leader's presence or lack of it.

The leader's aura should be 'open' and 'accepting'... no matter what. Anything else discourages discourse and violates the need for 'open' communications, which helps any project succeed. It allows for timely identification of possible issues or problems, that may need to be addressed immediately. To ensure this, a leader should attempt to be available, accepting and constructive in his or her comments, and never condemnatory or negative.

The key is to 'encourage' communication, not to stifle it. Communication is the lifeblood of any activity.

An 'open door' policy encourages 'walk-ins'. The project will often benefit from such openness.

If the leader adopts an off-putting, arrogant, self-involved attitude, then adequate communication will often suffer, as will the project.

We will not discuss 'body language' in this book in any thorough sense, although we may allude to it occasionally.

It does not take much for any perceptive person to pick up on body signals that radiate, 'leave me alone' or 'I am not interested'. That is a great way to turn off people who may need further instructions or who may wish to relay to the leader something of consequence or importance.

Keeping one's door ajar, allowing for entry and interruption, gives a very positive signal that entry is expected, appreciated and encouraged, except for those few occasions where no interruption is encouraged because of the need to accomplish one's own tasks, or to manage stress.

Part 1: Characteristics of a Good, Effective Leader

<u>Clear Communication</u>

Every leader MUST be able to communicate the leader's (project's or corporate) goals clearly and frequently. This is usually done at weekly meetings, but may require more frequent repetition, if and when necessary. The frequency of staff meetings is really determined by the experienced rate of change of the activity. For technical development it probably is very close to what is stated above, but for more static activities it my not require weekly meetings, as little changes in a one week or even a two-week period.

It is very important to emphasize both long-term and short-term goals, so that the team is always aware of upcoming milestones and more distant milestones. This also presents an opportunity to demonstrate how achievement of short-term goals is necessary to the fruition of long-term goals. The team must achieve both to truly be successful. Usually, achievement of short-term goals will help materialize long-term goals because the team is focused on both, without losing sight of either. Usually, long-term goals are nothing more than a collection of sequential short-term goals.

Achievement of short-term goals gives the team confidence that the long-term goals are achievable. Building confidence is very important. It is re-assuring.

When I was a much younger man in high school, I ran cross-country and I ran long distance. I was pretty good at it, although some others were better still. I found that the secret to success was never to concentrate on the long-term goal of running 2.5 to 5.0 miles but instead to concentrate on more immediate and more achievable goals. So, I concentrated on each step. Remember what Confucious is thought to have said (paraphrased): 'A long journey starts with the first step.' I forced myself to concentrate only on the runner immediately in front of me. Beating him would ensure first that the course was completed and second, by beating that runner, I'd not concentrate on the pain that I'd have to overcome to maintain such a fast pace. Further, in achieving my short-term goal, I was able to achieve my long-term goal, almost as an extra reward. The real effort was in achieving my short-term goals.

I have applied this rule to my own career and found that it applies equally. It allows focus and concentration to develop…necessary ingredients for any measure of success.

However, when leading others towards a common goal, it is often necessary to repetitiously reinforce the necessity of achieving goals that are short-term and within sight. It is easier that way. That is one of the Team Leader's goals. He or she maintains the team's focus where it ought to be: on achieving short-term milestones, on the way to overall success.

The team members should be aware at all times what he or she is expected to achieve within a given time frame. This is why the monitoring and achievement of milestones is so very important. That is also why milestones must be defined in no more than 2-week increments. Less than two weeks is very desirable but not always attainable. Beyond two weeks leaves too much time to be wasted, with negative project schedule and cost impact, and less chance of project recovery. Achieving a goal that only lies a few weeks away is much easier to focus on and to achieve than one that lies a year in the distant future.

Part 1: Characteristics of a Good, Effective Leader

I'd often require weekly status reports ahead of each week's staff meeting. The staff meeting was usually held on Monday mornings, to set the pace and tone for the remainder of the week. The status reports were usually sent to me by Noon Friday, with a meeting agenda sent out by C.O.B. that same day. Hence, when team members showed up at the Monday meeting, all knew what to expect. At the conclusion of the meeting, it was the PM leader's job to generate and distribute the Meeting Minutes by C.O.B. Monday for all team members to read and to take action on. More is said about this later in this book.

I have often pulled aside a team member, off-line, who has expressed a differing opinion to explain why the decision was made as it was. The usual reason was that the team members often only accounted for the technical impacts of an action, but not the contractual, cost or schedule impacts. This is the domain of the leader. And he or she needs to act and communicate accordingly.

A milestone-driven schedule is one of the few means of control given to a team leader. It should also be developed, committed to, understood, and used by the tasked individual, in order to bring about achievement of both short-term and long-term goals. It also allows identification of problem areas that may not have been foreseen at the development of the schedule. It therefore allows for swift corrective action, on the part of the team member or the Task Manager/Leader. The same is true of corporate or sales goals. Hence, it allows for the higher level schedule to be more nearly adhered to and achieved with timely correction, if needed.

The key again is understanding of both the short-term and the long-term goals. It requires understanding of the individual task milestones. If the goal is improved sales, then the immediate (weekly or monthly) sales projections must be achieved on the way towards meeting the annual sales goals. None of this is difficult to understand, but amazingly, such simple concepts are often overlooked in the fury of getting things done. Common sense is 'not so common' as one might believe.

Goals must be understood both by the tasked individual and the task leader, and perhaps even by the project leader. In any case, communication of these goals at all levels is highly necessary, if success is to be achieved.

This is true whether we are talking about technical development projects or sales projects. Communication is still very necessary. The frequency is determined by the pace of the task at hand. Communication may have to occur more than once a week or less than once a week, depending on the rate of change of the assignment.

An outstanding speaker and a co-founder of one company I worked for often gave highly technical seminars. To paraphrase what he said, it was something to the effect, that "if you say it often enough, to the point where you may think you are being repetitious, you are probably saying it about as often as is really needed." The same is true of reminding the team of its schedule and milestone commitments. Repetition ensures that the team members will easily recall their schedule committments.

Only then is success possible.

Part 1: Characteristics of a Good, Effective Leader

Customer Relations

This is another important topic. Without customers, there is no project, no sales and no work. To keep the customer in the communication loop in technical development projects, usually requires some kind of weekly phone call and/or monthly status report. This certainly seems fair enough.

In the case of Retail Sales, the begging questions to the customer become: "How can I help you?" or "What need can I help you with?" or even, "What do you plan to use this for?" The answers to these and similar questions allows one to truly give the customer what he or she truly seeks. The customer, whether in technical development or in Retail Sales may not be informed enough to fully know how to solve a particular problem, but they usually do know what problem they are attempting to solve. Solve the customer's problem and that customer will return again and again, because they have been treated with respect and their problem has been solved. The customer feels that his concerns have been heard and the recipient is attentive and attempting to assist the customer. This usually results in a satisfied customer, and increased sales, in the long run.

A 'good' leader recognizes this simple fact and marshalls his team to recognize it also. The results can be phenomenal and sales can sky-rocket, as a result. All that is required is that the team become aware of this. Usually, the leader will communicate this fact to the team on a regular basis. He or she may even sound repetitious at times but the end result is renewed focus on the customer's needs. All want the customer to return for additional business and sales. It means 'job satisfaction' and 'job security'. Recognizing the customer's true needs and not his or her 'perceived needs' is the ultimate answer and all team staff need to be conscious of this at all times.

To be complete, there is always an essential need to communicate with the customer, who is, after all, paying the bills or making the purchase.

For example, in a technical development project, there ought to be the transfer of a Statement of Work from the customer to the contractor, in response to the customer's original Request For Proposal (RFP).

The proposal is also available to the contractor. Such a proposal usually includes a WBS (Work Breakdown Structure), to collect and organize activities and their associated cost estimates, and any requirements for EVM (Earned Value Methods) reporting, along with cost and schedule plans. The proposal must also indicate all the project deliverables (documents, hardware, software), and how often status reviews are to be submitted.

In this case, the contractor ought to provide the customer with a system specification and a Compliance Matrix, whether or not they are defined within the contract. This ensures that all requirements are mutually understood by the development contractor and the customer. It also guarantees that the contractor is developing that which the customer requires or desires and not something different because of a misinterpretation of the requirements. These documents allow written confirmation, as understood by the contractor, of what is required by the customer. They allow real feedback from both sides. To ensure agreement, signatures of approval are usually included on the cover page, so that all the interested parties are in agreement as to

Part 1: Characteristics of a Good, Effective Leader

what is to be developed, and how.

During a technical development, there may be many other expected plans requiring customer review such as Design Plans, Test Plans, Staffing and Organizational Plans, Security plans, Configuration and Document Control plans, etc. These provide the customer with much needed insight into how certain areas are to be addressed and developed by the contractor. Oftentimes, these plans require customer review and comment before the actual associated effort is initiated. After all, the customer wishes, rightfully so, to know what he or she is paying for and how one intends to spend the money he is responsible for.

Another item in technical development that ought to include the customer, and often does, is the technical review of preliminary, interim and final system and/or subsystem design and test approaches. This allows the customer to provide timely corrective input and feedback regarding the proposed approaches.

Testing methodologies is also very important for technical development projects. This is especially true with complex systems-on a-chip. Sometimes random noise generators are employed internally to allow Testability, Observability and Controllability, all of which are important when the access to internal parameters is limited.

Here the main concerns are what are termed Observability and Controllability. How exactly does one ensure that a complex chip or anything, for that matter, is working if there is no feasible way of examining the internals, without including such access and possibly test generators at the beginning of the chip design process? Similarly, control of the chip must be made available externally if there is to be any chance of technical success. Testability, without any consideration of Observability and Controllability is usually insufficient. These concerns can apply to <u>any</u> development, not just to complex chip design.

Hence, the same is true for any non-electronic development system, in other words, for any type of system. The stated and defined parameters need to be observable and controllable. This infers testability of the required parameters of the target system.

Beyond and including testing, the customer limits the scope of the effort....if not technically, then in terms of cost, schedule or contractual requirements.

It is most important to recall that 'the customer is always right, even when he or she is wrong.' Never ever argue with a customer. It is a losing game. Instead listen to their concerns. If still wrong, then try gentle persuasion.

It seems strange but 'money talks' and the one with the money is the customer. Hence, the customer is usually given a heavy weight and input on any matters associated with the customer's project...and that is how it ought to be!

Besides, alienation of one's customer is highly undesirable because with the customer's alienation goes that particular sale and any future sales. Not only that, one's reputation will become smeared, a situation that no business can afford!

Part 1: Characteristics of a Good, Effective Leader

Projected Self-Assurance and Confidence: Leadership Essentials

How can a Leader 'lead' a project team or a any team, if he or she fails to project self-assurance and confidence? The answer: he or she cannot do it! It is essential for any leader to exude these characteristics or qualities. Why? Because most people respond in like. When a leader fails to project a sense of confidence, that sense is picked up by the team members. They begin to lack confidence in the 'leader's' ability to 'lead' them to a successful conclusion. Success, confidence and the like are infectious. Others will pick up on the same sentiment, be it positive or negative.

When I was a practicing project manager (PM), I always found this little trick to be very effective. Another way of saying the same thing is expressed when one says 'Don't let 'em see you sweat." Soooo true!! Always project positivity! Stay cool, calm and confident, especially when the 'sharks are in the water.'

No matter what pressures one may feel, it is very important, even essential, to keep them to oneself. Do NOT let others see that you are worried or concerned. Transmission of any negative sentiments can be highly destructive. Morale can plummet…and with it goes any chance of successful completion of the task at hand. Negative morale can be like a 'cancer'…it eats its own. And it can eventually kill the host. Hence, it is of paramount importance to project positivity at all times, especially when under duress. That is the mark of true and real 'leadership'. A 'leader' must always remain 'unwavering', 'focused' and 'self-assured'.

I once knew of a very senior PM ('leader') who

was managing a project that was experiencing a 'cost overrun'. However, this massive project was technically very challenging, pushing the 'state of the technical art' in almost every area. It was a project that was worth many tens of millions of dollars.

Whenever I greeted him I'd ask how he was doing, almost every other day. His response was always the same. "Fantastic". Well, I knew better. I knew the truth. Nonetheless, it did not matter because he never ever let anyone know what problems he faced (which were many) each and every day. He did work many long, long hours in his attempt to address some of these issues. However, his team always remained positive and fully confident in ultimate success. It was mainly due to his own projected 'self-assurance' that enabled his team to remain confident of success. Had the PM not done that he'd have betrayed himself and undermined his entire project. The challenging project would most likely have failed miserably, through self-cannibalism.

Positive attitude is a 'force-multiplier', as any experienced person who has encountered 'leadership' and its unique challenges, will attest.

Infection is usually negative. However, infection with 'positivity', which results in a permeating sense of 'confidence', is actually a very good thing, that can ultimately end in the achievement of difficult, challenging goals and the ultimate success of the project, or in a dramatic increase in sales.

Why? Because the team is focussed, and confident that positive results will accrue. This sense of 'success' is transmitted, not only to the team, but to customers as well. The result can only be positive everywhere.

Part 1: Characteristics of a Good, Effective Leader

Decisiveness in Leadership

All 'good' leaders know that the ability to make decisions (good ones) is one of the characteristics that sets a 'leader' apart!

There is nothing that will cause loss of confidence in a leader more than unnecessary and frequent procrastination. It can make the leader look weak, and a "weak' leader will eventually fail!

However, a 'leader' must make many decisions each day, often in the absence of complete or even desired knowledge. A good experienced 'leader' has the ability to make decisions in the absence of knowledge. Any reasonable person can make a decision with all the facts in hand. That is easy. What is much more difficult is making decisions in the absence of complete knowledge. 'Good' decisions made by the leader demonstrate his or her 'good' judgement.

However, none of us are perfect. An occasional 'poor' judgement may occur. It is better to make what one might consider a 'bad' decision, than to make 'no' decision whatsoever. A bad decision may not be desirable, but it can always be corrected. 'No' decision makes one's team wonder and ponder. This in itself can be destructive because it can erode the leader's ability to lead. He or she is seen as vacillating and lacking in direction or purpose. That is NOT a good way for a 'leader' to be perceived.

Not only that, hesitation on the part of the leader leads to hesitation and doubt on the part of the team members. The program will slow, sales will drop and overall performance will suffer as a result.

Likewise, 'rash' decisions can be equally destructive if made frequently and consistently. A 'rash' decision is made too quickly and without due consideration of the known facts. There is a certain balance required that only effective experience can provide. That is why effective experience is so very, very important.

Which is worse?: A 'leader' who is so overwhelmed, or who lacks sufficient relevant experience, that he or she cannot make a decision, or a 'leader' who makes an unpopular or incorrect decision.

Well, it may surprise you, but the second 'leader' is actually the better of the two. Please, let me explain. A 'leader' who is so overwhelmed by his or her position and who cannot or will not make a timely decision is a bane and a curse to the team's ability to become successful. This lack of decisiveness is paralyzing, not only to the 'leader', but also to the team. The project and its 'leader' do not exist in a vacuum. It is more like a fish bowl. Everyone can see in. Everybody is watching. A 'leader's' lack of focus or conviction is quickly sensed by the team, and it may negatively affect the team morale. It will cause team members to start doubting themselves and the ability of the project to achieve its goals. if the leader cannot make a decision. He or she will appear weak, irresolute and lacking in conviction. How can such a 'leader' ask others to trust in his or her judgment, if he or she is indecisive, with the leader not even trusting his or her own judgement?

Remember: lead with real confidence, but maintain integrity. This principle will carry the leader far with success as his or her tangible legacy.

When I was in high school, many decades ago, *Hamlet* by William Shakespeare was required reading. However, I always had a real problem with this particular

Part 1: Characteristics of a Good, Effective Leader

play. I could never understand Hamlet's passivity or lack of action. To me, then and now, his inaction paralyzed him from any effective action. It has led me to write a poem about it, which appears in one of my poetry books entitled, *Ramblings*. The particular poem is entitled, *To Be Or Not To Be*. This same inaction and subsequent paralysis is exactly what can happen on any project or corporate assignment. For an individual this is a character fault, but to a 'leader', such paralysis can be deadly.

Any team can detect this lack of self-assurance. The leader must always fight this appearance or perception. One becomes what one is perceived to be...even when that perception is mistaken! Believe it or not, 'perception is actually more important than reality.' It is the 'optics' that count in most people's view. That is what they will remember.

As stated before, conviction and confidence, can be infectious, in either direction. The 'leader' must ensure that it is a 'positive', reinforcing or constructive infection and not a negative, destructive one that will destroy the team and its chance of success. Further, a good 'leader' also has learned to make difficult, timely decisions in the absence of complete (100%) knowledge. Usually, if a 'leader' possesses 50% of the complete data needed to make his or her final decision, at any given time, that should be enough to make a fairly good decision. A poor decision can always be corrected later. An excessively delayed decision can result in disaster, and it can cause certain time-dependent tasks to either slip or to not be completed in time, or even budget. A rash decision can cause the improper assignment of resources and also cause project disaster, if not corrected in a timely manner.

Inaction by a leader can demoralize a team, cause confusion, and ultimately end up in reduced revenue or sales.

As an example, let us talk briefly about the Civil

War Battle called Antietam by the north, and Sharpsburg, by the south. When General McClellan (Union) first arrived at Antietam, he knew that his military opponent, Robert E. Lee (Confederate) was en route. (He had intercepted a message from Lee's camp, unknown to Lee). As a result, McClellan knew in advance of Lee's military plans, a great military advantage. Further, upon McClellan's early arrival on the battlefield, McClellan first out-numbered Lee's forces by about five to one. Very favorable odds indeed. However, McClellan was a perfectionist. That wasn't good enough for him to announce an attack. He wanted 100% probability that his Union Forces would 'win', even with pre-knowledge of the enemy's strategy and with 5:1 odds in his favor. Most generals would have been very happy indeed with such favorable odds and knowledge on his side.

McClellan's personality required him to have <u>complete</u> knowledge prior to the battle...a virtual impossibility. As McClellan waited for more munitions, more troops, more guns, etc., Lee kept gathering his own Confederate men from various disparate geographical locations. When the battle finally started McClellan had whittled his superiority over Lee from 5:1 to 2:1. Lee was brilliant in moving those forces around to where they were needed at any given time. In the end, Lee left the terrible battlefield, not having lost, as proclaimed falsely by the Union, but because a strategic withdrawal made excellent military sense. He had to preserve his smaller army from annihilation. Because he was the first to leave the battlefield, he was falsely declared the loser. In truth, the battle was actually a 'military draw'. However, the moral of this true tale is that one can never expect to operate or to make decisions in circumstances that will guarantee the end result. Don't attempt to wait for perfection or completeness. Neither will ever happen. Such is the destiny

Part 1: Characteristics of a Good, Effective Leader

of mere mortals. This is true on projects, in sales, in war, and in life, in general. In other words, 'get used to it'. Plan and act accordingly. The key is action vs inaction.

Remember, 'everyone is watching' how you (as leader) handle new and unique situations. If overwhelmed, use 'creative procrastination' to move the lower priority tasks into the background, where they can help un-clutter the situation. In other words, set priorities to eliminate any unnecessary clutter (that will only impede 'good' and 'timely' decision-making). If these crises are handled well, even without full knowledge (a rare commodity indeed), the project or the assignment will usually be successful.

With that success, comes positive recognition from team members, corporate leaders, and the customer. In addition, such experiences 'anneal' the leader, allowing him or her to have gained valuable and pertinent experience for future application. As the 'leader', 'all eyes are on you.' Make sure that the assessment is positive, and inspiring to the team. Timely decisiveness is paramount to ultimate success.

Over time, one's reputation for making difficult but timely decisions will become your trademark and others will want to be associated with a leader who has proven that he or she exercises 'good' judgement consistently and they will want to be part of your winning team.

Part 1: Characteristics of a Good, Effective Leader

Honesty & Integrity: Necessary Characteristics of an Effective Leader

Few of us like to be intentionally deceived. It just leaves a bad taste in one's mouth. The same is true of any team member. Trained people are willing to follow a 'true' leader only if they have confidence or trust in, that leader.

There are many ways to win a team's trust. One way is to be sure that verbal and written dialogues are honest, and that integrity is always demonstrated by the 'leader', and mimicked by the team itself.

Tolerance or intolerance for anything flows down from those at the top. Any one who says otherwise is either a self-deceptive fool or he or she is simply inexperienced. The leaders always set the example to follow. Honesty must be expected at every level for true trust to develop. If deception is accepted at the top, it will be accepted below that level, because humans follow by example. Deception eventually is discovered, and when it is discovered, the leader is seen as "having no clothes". At that point, trust is irrecoverable.

A 'true' leader never reveals his own doubts or feelings of uncertainty to the majority. A team or a group does not seek uncertainty. It seeks only certainty. As the project or team leader, he or she may instead seek counsel with a few very-well selected confidants. This does not mean that a true leader should never admit publicly, and occasionally, to ever having made a mistake. It merely means that such honesty ought to be demonstrated rarely and occasionally only. Otherwise, confide in those closest to you...advisors who will keep your secrets. He or she can turn to advisors and demand their opinion.

However, a 'true leader' never pretends to know something that he doesn't. Such pretension is often seen through quite easily. This is seen as 'insecure' or 'lacking in confidence'.

If anything, the willingness to own up to any shortcomings often wins the respect of others, because humility and honesty are rated more highly than pretension itself.

Do not reveal 'your warts' unnecessarily. Most folks will respect the individual who is courageous enough to admit having made a public error. Again, it builds on one's sense of integrity, for all to see. It can only help the leader's image…not hurt it! Nonetheless, such honesty must be utilized judiciously and infrequently, to avoid any erosion of confidence among team members.

The Apache of southwestern New Mexico never allowed a known 'liar' to any counsel meetings. A 'liar' was never called forth in a trial, because his or her word could not be trusted. In addition, 'deceptive or untrustworthy' individuals could become disqualified for warrior apprenticeship (dihoke) because of the mistrust engendered by that individual among fellow warriors. Individuals known to be 'liars' or 'deceptive' in some manner, were also not allowed to become messengers, i.e. to carry life-saving information from one group of Apache to another. The Apache feared that an 'untrustworthy' individual could endanger the entire band.

So, to be a successful leader one has to be honest, and maintain one's integrity. One should also set the example for others to follow. This sets a standard of professional behavior among one's followers.

If something confidential is to be discussed the leader's office door should be closed and each swear to the

Part 1: Characteristics of a Good, Effective Leader

other that all confidences remain in that closed-door office. We are all human. Sharing confidences is a two way street, but the key is keeping the confidence to oneself. That is how trust is built. I have found, over many years, that one is usually treated in accordance with the way one treats others, whether they be supervisors or direct reports. Here the Golden Rule applies: "Treat others as you wish to be treated yourself.' So very true!

Remember: "Expected' values become 'real' values'. So, be sure to set the right tone of what your expectations are from the very start. That not only includes the project cost, schedule or technical performance issues, or perhaps sales/revenue goals, but the overall behavioral expectations of the leader and the team. Honesty breeds honesty; so too, for integrity. Unfortunately it is also true that 'deception at the top breeds deception at the bottom.' Avoid this at all cost!

If one wants to lead a team that is honest and trustworthy, then the leader must set that example. Also, such an environment, promulgated and established by the leader, gives other team members the sense that the leader can be trusted. At that point, they know that the leader will always try to be as honest as possible with them, and he or she will look out for their best interests. Such a leader can thereby form his or her own kind of charisma. With that, the team will do anything and go anywhere to ensure team success, and thereby everyone wins the game. The customer and the company executives are happy with a successful project or with 'met' sales and financial goals. So too are the leader and the team. By so doing, they accomplish what they set out to do. That gives great satisfaction. The team feels a sense of pride and accomplishment in having identified and having overcome the challenge placed before them.

Not only will the result be trust in the leader. it also

goes the other way too. If a leader has a dishonest team, how does he or she ever know when he or she is being told the truth about the status of a particular task? To properly manage a critical task or project it is essential that the status information being passed along to the leader is honest and truthful, at all times.

Perhaps better than a tabular presentation of financial or sales goals, it may be best to show a cumulative chart of performance achievement, so that the entire team can form an image of their performance and they can see it over time, as opposed to a single snapshot in time. Visual feedback of this type allows for modification of the team's behaviour and a sincere desire to meet the visual goals. It engenders pride among team members.

In the end, both the leader and the team realize that each needs the other, for true success to occur. It truly is a cooperative effort! Needs are met through trust, honesty, integrity and confidence. Faith in each other is essential. These qualities are 'the stock from which the soup is made.' Without honesty and integrity, there can be no trust or confidence in the leader. The team will be working at cross-purposes, and inevitably this will lead to 'failure'...not success.

Part 1: Characteristics of a Good, Effective Leader

Posture and Leadership

Not often does one see these two topics together! However, the truth is that posture is very important, especially for a leader. Posture often reflects outwardly what one feels inwardly. Victims tend to walk with stooped shoulders and with poor posture. They also tend to look 'weak' or 'powerless'. They look more like 'prey' and they often become so, in large part, because of their own negative and 'victim-like' projection or poor self image. 'A person is what one projects'. This is true to a great extent about almost any aspect of life.

'Power' projects itself. It also projects 'surety' and 'confidence'. People respond to that. Folks seek leadership and they usually seek out 'positive', 'competent', 'hopeful' and 'confident' people to follow. They usually do not follow cowards, negative thinkers or those who project 'lack of confidence'. It is not the human way. 'Leaders' know this, often instinctively. That is why 'leaders' usually demonstrate 'good posture'. Believe it or not, it is a 'power' statement. How many leaders have you known with very 'poor' posture, with' sloping shoulders' and bellies that protrude beyond their chest?

My father was never one of them, posture-wise, although he, like so many others put on a bit too much around the waist as he grew into old age. I remember my father, who served in WW2, telling me, as a young boy, "shoulders back, back straight, stomach in, chin in, chest out…always." I have never forgotten that instruction to this very day. It is a great direction to give anyone, especially an aspiring leader. 'You are what you project'. A leader must always, under any and

Thoughts On Leadership

all circumstances, project 'confidence', 'trust', 'experience', 'capability', etc. How one carries oneself physically, reflects either a sense of or a lack of confidence.

It is important to think about how others see you. You want to come across as experienced, confident, i.e., as a 'winner'. Very few people will follow a 'loser'. It is human nature, and perhaps even animal nature, to follow a 'winner'. It certainly seems so in primitive societies and among the animals in the animal world. 'Betas' (non-dominants) follow an 'alpha' (a dominant) of any species, including humans.

Regarding humans, it makes folks believe that they have chosen to be on the 'right' side. What really happens is less important than what they believe will happen. Many great leaders exhibit an upright posture because they are confident in themselves. They project 'alphaness'. They may or may not be aware of what they do in this regard. It may almost be instinctive, but true nonetheless.

Great posture projects an image of strength, of purpose, and of good health. If one were to follow a great leader, one assumes that the leader is healthy enough to be around for a long while. No one wishes to follow an unhealthy leader, because the individual cannot project health, and further may not be around long enough to complete the assigned task. Why not follow another who will be around?

Regardless of what one's politics are, one needs to examine the 'body language' of each candidate as well as the 'verbal' responses, which are usually untrue, and meant to garner votes. The real message is to be found in the 'non-verbal' arena.

Of all the candidates who were running for either party during the 2016 Presidential Primaries, only one projects poor posture and a lack of confidence. I am not here to play political games. I will leave it to the reader to

Part 1: Characteristics of a Good, Effective Leader

figure out who that individual may be. I have always been a believer in watching what one does to see if what he or she says is compatible with what one does. The latter is the true parameter to monitor. Demagogues often tell the public what it wants to hear but he or she will usually do the very opposite, as he or she gathers power in often 'legal' but unscrupulous ways. 'Legal' is not the same as 'moral'.

Not only that, the deed is usually done when few will notice: in the evening, on a Friday, over a weekend, when other events will crowd it out. The hope is that the individual may not take notice of it. This is deception at work, and should be seen as such.

Another important aspect of leadership is 'tone'. We are either blessed or not with a deep authoritative voice. Some are not so blessed. I, for one, do not have a deep voice. I try to make up for this deficiency by means of my upright posture and my self-assurance. However, deep voices, and 'low frequencies' often are soothing and comforting. Think of relaxation methods. One may have to make the 'ohm' sound. Why? Because it is a low frequency which causes us to relax. Perhaps, it is because the frequencies are low enough that they approach the frequency of human resonance. We are, without a doubt, both physical and spiritual beings. So, physical resonance is true of our physical bodies just as surely as it is for any other physical body. During intense relaxation, one can sometimes feel one's body seek synchronization with that self-resonance frequency.

If one has such a voice one should use the deep tones in a natural way to enlist the support and allegiance of others. Otherwise, try to learn to speak in a low voice, where possible, without looking or sounding ridiculous. As with all things, do it 'in moderation' as the wise, ancient Greeks once discovered. It should sound natural; otherwise, never mind, because it is better to be and to appear honest and sincere. In summary, one's being and one's projection are out there for all to see. Since that is true, it is essential to project positivity, confidence, integrity, competence, experience and assuredness. That is why a great leader uses every tool available to him or her, in order to solicit support and to exude leadership that others fight to follow.

Again, this is exactly how animals respond to an 'alpha' of their own species, in their presence. Based on this similarity, there really must be something scientific and real about what is being said here.

Part 1: Characteristics of a Good, Effective Leader

How You Show Your Hands

I have written much about management and leadership. Here, in this discussion, I wish to touch on something that is important to any speaker or any leader. I wish to talk about 'hands'. What has that got to do with leadership, you confusedly ask?

Well, you might be very much surprised to learn that one's use of hands is vital to leadership or even speaking. For example, it is a veritable 'no-no', at any time and under any circumstance, to 'point one's finger (s) at another'. It is most often seen as 'aggressive, belligerent and unnecessarily authoritative'.

Sounds right to me. I, in my long experience tried never to do this. However, I was pointed at once, in a 'threatening, cocky' manner by a nearby individual in a Configuration Control department in one of several companies that I had once worked for. Needless to say, I took it as a very aggressive action and that individual never tried that again…at least not with me. The moral here is: Do Not Point Fingers at Another Individual. It is 'negative, demanding and provocative.' It may even lead to an undesired physical encounter.

There is another hand action that can be either bad or good, depending upon the manner in which it is 'handled'. (Punny, I know, but what the hay!) If a speaker wishes to make a point, never, ever use 'down-pointing fingers, palms or hands. This action is often perceived as 'demanding' or even 'commanding'. It is seldom received 'openly'. Instead, it comes across as 'closed to discussion'. Try to communicate with open hands, i.e. with hands extended but with palms 'up', rather than 'down'. Generally, audiences and staff often perceive such an action as 'open-minded, worthy of consideration.'

It is all in how one shows one's hands. 'Palms up' equals openness and a willingness to listen and consider. 'Palms down' is perceived as closed-minded, with an unwillingness to listen or consider other viewpoints.

It is very important to realize that verbal communications represent only 10% of what one human communicates to another. The remaining 90% is via 'body language'. Hence, un-uttered, non-verbal actions are commonly and easily read by many, even if they are not aware of it or why. Every speaker or leader must know at least the rudiments of 'body language' to fully succeed.

There is one more action that I wish to discuss here, and that is 'fingers pensively touching the lips'. We have all seen it and most of us have also done it. The speaker or the leader, casually puts his or her index finger to his or her lips. Usually, such an action is viewed upon as 'considering, pensive, open to suggestion.' Again, it is usually perceived in either a 'neutral' or a 'positive' light. Use this action selectively however. Otherwise, if it occurs too often, it can be then perceived as 'indecisive or uncertain'. A leader must always be perceived as 'decisive'. Therefore, this action should be used very sparingly, so that the message does not become one of general 'indecisiveness'.

Animals are experts at reading non-verbal cues. After all, is that not how they communicate, together with a few other sounds, such as grunts, or growls? Animals, generally, have no verbal vocabularies. They rely heavily upon non-verbal cues to 'get it'. We are more like animals than we care to admit, but in assigning ourselves over the animals, we place too much emphasis on 'verbal' cues and not enough emphasis on 'non-verbal' cues. Leaders need

Part 1: Characteristics of a Good, Effective Leader

to be aware of both. I always know, as most pet owners do, when my dogs are hungry, ashamed, happy, sad, depressed, angry, threatened, etc. In general, I certainly don't get this impression from their speech, although their vocal sounds can alert me to their mood too. They can tell, from body language alone, whether someone is a threat or not. Although I can detect the same at times, I am not as consistent as they are.

My wife says that I know 'dogspeak'. Maybe! I have had one dog type or another for more than 55 years. All I do is watch them and interact with them. I even respond by howling back when they first see me. Sounds crazy, huh? All I know is that it helps me bond more closely with them... and I think they know it too. I know they are happy and they make sure that I know too. They wag their tails. Their faces look like they are smiling. They make unique sounds. They jump up and down, seeking a pat or some other attention. They simply exercise body language. After I greet them, give them some affection and attention, they then settle down.

As humans, we are capable of so much more than any animal. Yet, we need to remember that the most 'honest' communication comes from our non-verbal responses…not our verbal responses. It is sort of like the saying: 'they'll tell you what you really want to hear.' That statement shows the inherent unreliability in verbal responses. Even when you hear what you want to hear, it doesn't mean that you are hearing the Gospel truth. On the other hand, body cues can often reveal such intentional or unintentional truths, or even a visible reluctance to do or say something.

This is not a book about 'body language'. However, the few points given here are very important and they should be the very minimum known to the speaker or leader. There is however, still much, much more.

Thoughts On Leadership

Part 1: Characteristics of a Good, Effective Leader

Murphy's Law and What You See Is What You Get

I wish to talk briefly here about two other management principle that are evident to some but not to others. These are, as the title above suggests, 'Murphy's Law and What You See is What you Get.' What do I mean by that statement?

First, let us address the notorious Murphy's Law. It is just not in the true nature of things to have everything run perfectly and smoothly. If so, why then are leaders ever needed. The project or sales projection could then easily be put on 'autopilot', and the project would also cost less, or the sales projection would be easily realized since no senior leadership is required.

The so-called 'Murphy's Law' always applies to reality. "If anything can go wrong, it will...at the most inopportune time."

I don't know who Murphy was, but he was certainly very wordly and knowledgeable about real life. The statement above is very true and very fitting for real life situations. The morale: Plan for (expect) things to go wrong but hope for the best outcome. Never plan optimistically. You most often will be sorely disappointed. Murphy did not gain acclaim because he was wrong, but the reverse. Hence, things will most likely go wrong. Plan for it. Make sure that a great captain is at the helm when troubled times and events occur, which they inevitably will. On the other hand seize opportunities and re-plan as necessary when these land happily in your lap. They may help you recover from an occurrence of Murphy's Law.

Everyone wishes to win.

Now, let us address the second topic: What You See

is What You Get. This concerns one's attitude as projected by the leader. An attitude of 'failure' and of 'lacking confidence' will doom any effort, large or small. It is very important to always remember that teams follow whomever they believe are 'winners'. Everyone wants to be part of a winning team. No one wants to be associated with a 'loser'.

Projection is everything. If this is true then the only projection that is desirable and that will produce success is one of positivity and confidence. This theme is presented throughout this book because it is so important that repetition is worthwhile.

How one presents oneself, is what one gets. Hence, it is important to project oneself positively and effectively. Project what you wish others to perceive.

Projected negativity will materialize as failure, which is highly undesirable.

Remember: "What you see is what you get." It is much more important than many realize!

Part 1: Characteristics of a Good, Effective Leader

Credibility

A true leader has to be someone that others can trust. It is very important to be perceived as 'credible' and 'trustworthy' and to be seen as 'in earnest'. Without such credibility, there is no trust and without trust the risk of project failure increases exponentially. How can a team follow someone they cannot trust? They cannot because they need to follow someone they have faith and confidence in. Otherwise, failure is the usual outcome. Integrity is also very important.

What is integrity? It is the willingness to stand up to others for what one believes. Integrity means consistency and 'good' character. It takes a certain courage to maintain integrity in the face of opposition...even corporate opposition! It may require 'standing up' to one's own corporate management. Often, this may come at great personal and professional cost, since no one wishes to be challenged, especially by those 'on top' who may see such a challenge as a threat. You may be respected for your courageous stand but punished, nonetheless. Power, never wants to look bad, even when the 'power wielders' are wrong.

I have always held my own integrity as paramount to my being...never the corporate ladder. Many of my peers and co-workers respected me, and I believe that many of my own bosses did too....but secretly. I advanced in spite of my integrity and honesty. It doesn't often happen that way. Even the senior V. P. said of me at my Retirement, attended by many folks from various departments in the company, that: "John never cared much what upper management ever thought, he just did what he felt was right." True! That is how

Thoughts On Leadership

I believe everyone should act...with integrity, because it is the only way to maintain credibility. It is also the only thing that one can always call one's own!

When I was much younger I listened to a vinyl LP (now I am really showing my age) in which there was a folk song that asked "who'd you rather trust, the hawk or the dove?" The answer is the hawk. Why? Because with the hawk, one always knows what it will do. I tried never to be untruthful, even if my statements went against the corporate view. I figured that I was not being paid, with all my many decades of experience, to tell what was desired but to tell the truth, as I saw it. It was difficult to do at times because of the pressure brought to bear on me, especially from my management. However, I always managed to hold out...it was important to me to be honest and forthright. By so doing, I garnered a reputation for not being a 'yes' man and for being honest and credible, not only among team members but among the corporate staff. It was dicey but fortunately I had superiors who respected that personal and professional characteristic.

These are all important essentials for any leader who wishes to succeed and who wishes to move his team towards 'force multiplication.' Only then can the 'whole be greater than the sum of its parts.' The team needs something and someone to follow, to lead them towards successful implementation of a real challenge. They need to look up to their leaders. This cannot be if there is no respect for the leader, because the leader chooses never to keep his or her word. This character flaw in the leader will very quickly be seen by the team. 'Honesty' and 'credibility' are usually the best policy. It's an old adage but true nonetheless.

It is very difficult to remember all the lies once spoken. Eventually, the lies will be discovered and then trust

Part 1: Characteristics of a Good, Effective Leader

in the leader will have vanished for evermore. Trust cannot easily be rebuilt once that trust is violated. The team will always question what the leader says versus what he or she does. Once shattered, the leader's ability to lead becomes compromised by his or her own deceit or deception.

Be flexible and DO NOT POINT BLAME on anyone. That is a child's game! Figure out what is wrong and fix it, do not try to find blame. It is irrelevant. It belongs where it occurred...in the past.

Assigning blame does nothing but cause the staff to become defensive instead of concentrating on how to solve a specific problem. It is the 'solution' one seeks, not blame or punishment. Pointing blame is usually done by someone who is insecure or inexperienced. Avoid this terrible tactic, whenever possible. No one likes to be publicly admonished for a mistake in judgment. We all are capable of making such mistakes.

Another point: It is never a good idea to just reprimand a staff member with negativities. Instead, show how the staff person is needed, and is an important member of the 'team'. It is important for that individual to know how he or she has made positive contributions, and that those same contributions are recognized and acknowledged by the leader. Then bring up areas for improvement...not a scolding! Just mention what could be done in a better way or with another's help. And do it one on one....never in a group setting, where the staff person can become embarrassed, nervous, defensive and feel like he or she is being unfairly attacked. Never chastise, if possible. Instead, encourage behavioral change.

The morale of your team is most important to achieve success. Seek to make your team into 'a well oiled machine.' Remember: always look forward to the future...

it can be changed. The past is already done and it surely cannot be changed. Accept that reality and move forward in a constructive, positive way.

Another important thing to remember: 'One is only as good as one's word.' It may sound corny in today's age, but it is eternally true, regardless.

'Keep on leading until the goal is achieved.' Only then should the team celebrate and take some time to relax, while patting itself on the shoulders for a 'job well done!'

Part 1: Characteristics of a Good, Effective Leader

<u>Necessary Essentials:</u>
<u>Mutual Respect & Genuine Humility</u>

Two very important essentials for any leader or project manager are mutual respect and a sense of sincere humility. These elements can make a leader come across as 'charismatic.' Charisma is very important in terms of being able to motivate staff to do the leader's or the project's bidding. One has to appeal to one's self image. One has to be able to tap into one's inner need for achievement of difficult goals. (It builds confidence and experience). Charisma is one way to do so.

Nothing great is ever achieved by a leader with a huge 'ego' and nothing else. Most leaders do have big 'egos'. However, the real question is whether the leader lets his own ego dictate circumstances and approaches or whether the 'leader' is confident enough to listen to his reports when they have something useful or even 'earthshattering' to say. This boils down to having an obvious respect for the 'doers'. It is important that the team show respect to the leader but it is equally important for the leader to show respect for the opinion of others. It is a two-way street. 'Give and ye shall receive' is a famous old adage that turns out to be true! To gain true respect, to the point where others will deny themselves in order to ensure the success of the project requires showing respect to others in a mutual way. Give credit where it is due...publicly and frequently.

Hence, not only does the leader 'respect' others, he or she must project a genuine sense of humility. It must be genuine because if it is not, the staff will quickly detect it...if not the first time, then certainly by the second time.

Self-deprecation does not diminish the 'leader'. Instead, it shows that the 'leader' is 'human' and does not take himself or herself too seriously. If the 'leader' is always worried more about his or her image, the shallowness will eventually become very apparent. No one wants to follow someone who is arrogant and self-absorbed. Confident yes, arrogant, no!

Learn to laugh at oneself. It will be appreciated but do it sparingly so as to maintain one's positive image. When one learns to be self-deprecating, others see that the 'leader' does not see oneself as flawless, and unerring, but as a normal human being doing one's best. It makes it a lot easier to offer positive and constructive comments on another's performance if indeed the 'leader' is truly humble.

Also, it is important to have a sense of humor. After all, there is usually much that is not humorous...problems galore (from 'gu leoir', Sc. Gaelic). However, a little levity makes it a little easier for everyone to get through the day and to succeed because the fear of 'failure' is diminished. Instead, the team can concentrate on doing their tasks successfully and without fear.

Occasional levity breaks the stress of any given situation. Use it, but use it wisely. Do not allow yourself to come across as a light-hearted 'fool' either. That will not serve the leader or the assignment well.

When I was managing some very difficult projects, I would always say the following: 'A smile costs nothing but it can produce enormous positive results.' I always tried to listen to other approaches and to other opinions and to implement the best one, even if it was not my idea. I also tried to give credit to the fine efforts of my various fantastic technical teams. After all, if I were to take all the credit for a project success, it not only comes across (rightly) as arrogant and self-absorbed, it does not fairly recognize that

Part 1: Characteristics of a Good, Effective Leader

the project or assignment success was not only due to the application of good leadership principles, but also to the superlative efforts of many talented and hard-working staff members. Most people want to succeed in whatever they do. As a leader, one needs to 'tap into' this desire and direct it towards achievement of the project or corporate goals.

Most folks want to be associated with a 'winner'. They wish either to be part of a winning team and/or to work with a winning leader, because then that individual can share in the achievement of difficult goals and thereby participate in the project's or the corporate success. When this happens it is most important to share the 'glory' with those who made it possible. Nothing happens by itself. 'Teamwork' is what makes the big difference, and 'teamwork' only comes about when, among other things, the leader shows respect to his team members (and vice versa) with a sense of real humility! Only then can they work together and synergistically to achieve the project or corporate goals.

A 'team' if properly led, can become an entity unto itself, with its own discipline, its own requirements, its own behaviour, its own memory and its own 'esprit de corps'. They will all eventually remember similar shared 'war stories' and 'battle scars' that only they can relate to. Once that happens, the group or team develops a 'collective' memory, that only they who have experienced the trials and tribulations can identify with. They become 'one'. Each wants the other to succeed because they all share the same outcome.

Recognize that as a 'leader' you cannot and will never 'know everything'. Accept this simple fact and act accordingly. If so, 'humility' will follow naturally. Show respect to those who report to you. Chances are they know a lot that you, as the leader, do not. Encourage discussion and different viewpoints, consider them as needed, accommodate them if they make sense. Do not come across as so thin-skinned that you do not accept an idea because it originated with someone else. If the idea is a good one, laugh it off by saying, "Wow. That's a great idea. I don't know why I never thought of that!" Remember: Success is a 'team' effort! It is not an individual effort!

Diversity of opinion is what brings about breakthroughs and momentous change...not the status quo!

Hence, it is always wise to encourage the expression of different viewpoints and approaches. It is often called 'out of the box' thinking. By all means, encourage it. The assignment or project may achieve a 'breakthrough' because of it.

Working together, with respect and a proper sense of humility, can often help bring about project or corporate success, that everyone can be proud of...the team members and the team leader.

Part 1: Characteristics of a Good, Effective Leader

Being Bold & Persistent

A timid leader rarely succeeds. Being a 'true' leader, often requires a propensity towards 'boldness' and the need to take timely, strong and decisive action. Success rarely gathers around those who are too reluctant or too timid to 'act' when that is the only correct thing to do. It requires a certain decisiveness, essential to any leadership role.

It requires 'seizing' opportunities when they occur. If this does not happen promptly, the opportunity can quickly disappear, leaving the hesitant holding an empty bag. In other words, without acting boldly and promptly, the opportunity can quickly vanish and disappear. 'Opportunity only knocks once', as they say. Grab it when at all possible...and do it quickly.

An inexperienced leader may make a decision that is too precipitous. Experience is the factor that decides when to 'act' and when 'not to act'. We discussed the importance of 'experience' earlier in this book. We will address it once again in another chapter. It is still clearly important, but just as important is the quality of 'bold and timely action'.

Look to many of the great military leaders in history. In almost every case, success was attached to the leader who was able to see opportunities that others could not see, and then, just as importantly, they acted swiftly and even, brazenly, when they recognized the opportunity. One can easily recall the actions of Julius Caesar, Alexander the Great, Hannibal, Robert E. Lee and many, many other great military leaders.

The lesson could not be clearer. Fate favors the bold!
Every leader needs to have back-up plans. These plans

should be 'living' documents that get updated and modified regularly. By being flexible and by exploiting any new and unforeseen opportunities that may arise spontaneously, the leader can often succeed. Oftentimes, the opportunity quickly vanishes and therefore 'bold, decisive action' is essential if there is to be any chance to seize the unforeseen opportunity.

One benefit that is often overlooked is the effect that such wise use of 'boldness' has upon the morale of the team that is following the 'leader'. Such decisiveness enhances the view of the team upon the capabilities of the 'leader'. It boosts confidence, unless the 'leader' is reckless. As I have said many, many times before, success is infectious and others always wish to follow a 'winner', rarely a 'loser'.

Bold action only enhances a positive image of the leader. Inaction, on the other hand, often causes demoralization among the team. No room for the paralytic Hamlet or his like here.

Knowing this, every 'leader' should be unafraid to make rationally considered but momentous decisions and 'bold' moves. The key is to have pre-prepared answers to the question, What if...? These decisions and bold actions can result in unexpectedly successful results. Nonetheless, wise 'bold' action can turn a potentially troubled project into a raving success...but it requires a level of intuition that usually comes about from a sufficiency of experience.

Every decision requires a certain level of confidence or assurance. An experienced 'leader' can usually make such decisions easily and quickly, whereas an inexperienced 'leader', can often miss the opportunity, or he or she may not act quickly or assuredly enough to be effective. Inexperience often causes hesitation and 'self-doubt.' Such hesitation can be fatal and lead to a lack of success.

Part 1: Characteristics of a Good, Effective Leader

The 'leader' must be 'brave'. It allows him or her to become bold, as necessary.

To allow 'boldness' to flourish, the 'leader' cannot be phlegmatic, or listless. Instead, the true 'leader' must be brave, decisive, and effective. However, he or she must also have considered the consequences, should his or her decision turn out to have been incorrect. What happens if the assumptions used in making the decision prove untrue or incorrect?

Here, 'back up' plans can help rescue the consequences of the poor decision.

Thoughts On Leadership

Part 1: Characteristics of a Good, Effective Leader

The Significance of Effective Experience

Effective experience is often overlooked as significant by too many. Many people like to 'take someone on faith' alone, to adhere or listen to their promies. Promises certainly indicate good intentions. However, I'd rather see whether the good intentions result in any effective, productive, related action. If not, the promise means nothing. If so, then the promise is worthy.

I contend that 'good intentions' alone are inadequate and fraught with all kinds of danger. For one thing it places 'entire' control in the hands of the other, with none for oneself. It matters not what one's intentions are if one cannot show evidence of an ability to execute. They are not the same thing. One is 'hope' without any backup; the other is proof that the individual is 'likely' to succeed based upon hard evidence from past experiences.

Experience without concrete 'successful results' is really meaningless, because the person could have been doing things incorrectly for ages, and that is why there are no visible results to show for the expended effort.

When I lived in California, decades ago, I had bought several boxes of blue randomly speckled ceramic tiles. The boxes (3) were all from the same die lot. I had a contractor come to lay them on the upstairs bathroom floor. I checked with him three times a day to ensure that he was implementing the work as I had specified. One day, I came home at lunch time to inspect his work and to ensure that all was well. I worked close to my home at the time, so that was not a problem. He had already taken the tile out of the three boxes and he had blindly laid them with mastic onto the floor about an hour before I had arrived. He had just applied the tiles as they came out of the box, with no thought applied nor any visionary check. When I saw the floor, I got very upset. I asked him whether he ever did a 'dry lay' before he applied the mastic. His answer was "no". The tile floor looked blotchy and very unprofessional. I asked him, "Did you ever look at this to see if it was visually pleasing?" I also asked him, "How long have you been doing this?" He answered "Twenty-five years." I responded with, "Well you have been doing it incorrectly for all that time. Just look at it. It's terrible." "But they are all the same die lot." He responded. In truth, they were all the same die lot but anyone with half a brain could see that the floor looked blotchy. No common sense was being applied here. Fortunately, the mastic had not yet set, I told him to remove all the tile and I would "dry-lay' them that evening myself. He did so, and I went back to work.

That evening, I alternated (dry-lay) the tile so that those that were darker alternated with those that were lighter. It looked great when I finished. Since there were not an equal number of darker and lighter tiles, I selected the remainder to be put under the bathroom vanity where they'd not be seen. I showed him the layout next day and he implemented my approach, to my satisfaction.

What did I learn from this unpleasant experience? Many decades of experience means nothing if the result is unsatisfactory, incomplete or wrong!

So, whenever anyone touts a great deal of experience, I am usually unimpressed until I learn of the results of such effort and experience. If it was successful with concrete results, fine. Else, I am not impressed.

I knew of several young, ambitious individuals who had gotten fancy MBA's or Master's in Project Management,

Part 1: Characteristics of a Good, Effective Leader

but with very little practical experience. This case was mentioned briefly in the Introduction. It is re-introduced here in more detail.

They impressed their bosses because of the advanced degrees they had achieved. Good in itself but not enough! A degree is 'book learning'. In no way can it substitute for real life experience, where the individual may have failed or witnessed others who have failed. These failures are better 'learning' exercises than can be obtained from any book. Needless to say, the neophytes with their advanced degrees failed miserably, whereas some older, more experienced leaders, without the Master's Degrees, did much better. The neophytes may have eventually ended up as fine leaders, but at the time their advanced degrees did not help them. They simply were not ready...they had not obtained enough practical effective experience.

I have always found, personally, that I have learned the most through failures, sometimes through my own, more often from the failures of others. It is not our successes from which we learn but through our disappointments and failures.

Corporate executives 'love' to see 'experienced' people assigned to a project because it instills them with confidence. They can safely assume that if an 'experienced' leader has pulled off a difficult but similar project in the past, the 'likelihood' of a repeat performance is high. They can never say the same about someone who is 'inexperienced' or is somehow an 'unknown' quantity. Again the critical criteria is 'success' not just experience alone.

Customers love effective experienced leaders for the same basic reason. It provides the best possible chance of success.

Teams want to follow 'proven, successful' leaders... not experimental ones. Their own futures are tied to the success of their leaders. Hence, it only makes good sense to seek out those with 'successful effective experience'. It can make all the difference in the world.

Experienced effective leadership not only motivates a team, it self-motivates the 'leader'. Because of such experience, there is very little hesitation, second or third guessing, etc. Confidence, based upon years of practical experience, allows greater, faster, more efficient decision-making. I always sought out individuals who knew more than I did, otherwise there is no way to learn. Learn from the 'effective experienced' ones; they have seen it all, and they have developed 'wisdom' not just 'knowledge'. Only personal experience can so 'anneal a leader'.

The objective of meeting the technical requirements, the financial funding and the schedule of any project can be more realizable with an 'effective experienced' leader. The same is true about achieving corporate sales objectives.

'Effective experience' means that difficult situations have already been encountered and dealt with, and hopefully 'learned from'. An 'inexperienced' leader has no such card under his or her sleeve. Much learning has still to be done, many mistakes have yet to be made, usually at the expense of individuals on the team and of the project or effort especially. Only after that does the 'real' wisdom come that is associated with 'experience'.

'Inexperience' usually leads to unsuccessful outcomes, whereas, 'effective experience' usually brings success as long as the other essential elements of good leadership are also implemented. Again, the experience must be associated with tangible successful results to be meaningful. A proven track record demonstrates just that.

I know what choice I'd make always: 'successful experience' over 'inexperience' any day of the week!

Pettinesss and Self-Defensiveness: Incompatible With Leadership

An attitude of 'pettiness', 'thin-skinnedness' or 'self-defensiveness' are negative qualities. Any of these, and several more are incompatible with great leadership. Why? Because the projected focus is first of all negative, not positive. Secondly, it means that the perceptive recipient of such gestures sees the leader as 'all about himself or herself', as the case may be.

This is exactly the opposite of what a great leader means to project. Instead, the projection should not be about 'self' but about the task or effort at hand.

All too often I have witnessed this shortcoming in otherwise 'good' leaders. It negatively affects team morale and it reflects negatively on the 'leader', who is seen as 'small minded' and 'thin-skinned' A good leader should be confident enough and experienced enough to take constructive criticism, as perhaps even helpful and observant, not as an attack on his or her person.

Defensiveness is usually either due to an inflated sense of self or it is because the individual lacks experience, and wishes not to be discovered.

If and when the criticism is widespread and may endanger the success of achieving the objective, then action is required. Even then it must be responded to quickly and firmly, so as not to undermine team morale. I have seen some naysayers constantly whine and complain, bringing the morale of an entire team down with it. This action by team-members cannot be tolerated either and should be addressed with resolution and timeliness to recover affected morale. If change is necessary, do not be afraid to look bad or to have changed one's mind. Make the change and let the naysayers try to undermine you after the change has been made, even as they themselves may have recommended. Remain above the fray not within it. A great leader has to rise above such pettiness, both in oneself and in others. In either case, too much tolerance is NOT a virtue, but instead it can be seen as weakness, requiring change or swift decisive action.

Once, while a Director, I was heading towards the rest room. I saw a Senior Engineer whining and complaining to other team members on a particular project about the difficulty he had been experiencing writing a certain technical specification. I had witnessed this numerous times before but I had sadly not taken timely action. However, on seeing this again, I decided to intervene.

I approached him and the others. They sensed a confrontation and quickly left, leaving just the two of us there. The Senior Engineer started to complain yet again. I quickly stopped him and I asked him the following question: "Are you a Senior Engineer or not?" He briefly answered "Yes." I then told him that any Senior Engineer has enough experience to complete the specification. Otherwise, he does not deserve the senior position.

Further, if there is an issue, the expectation of someone at his senior level is to identify the problem, offer several options, get together with me or someone else senior to him who will then work with him to choose the appropriate option/solution for him to address. After this 'friendly' scolding, I said that I expected him to act according to his senior level and not to act like a junior engineer. The result: the specification document was completed within the next two weeks, whereas formerly, the effort had languished for

Part 1: Characteristics of a Good, Effective Leader

several months. In some ways, I had allowed this effort to languish much too long. I should have acted sooner than I eventually did. Nonetheless, decisive action, although late in this case, resulted in a prompt termination of the undesired activity (whining, extended production of the document, negating the team morale, etc.) and a quick conclusion of the needed document generation.

A leader must never be perceived as 'weak', 'vacillating' or 'self-centered'. Any and all of these can be very destructive of achieving the main objective. The problem must never be about oneself or one's inadequacies. There may be a personality clash that causes the defensiveness too. Either way, the solution is to remove the cause of the contention, if it is impacting the progress of the project and its ultimate success. Again, in this instance, quick decisive and bold action is required to prevent the morale problem from becoming contagious to other team members.

The team seeks leadership, strong unwavering leadership. There is no room for self-doubt or self-defensiveness. It is perceived exactly for what it is: uncertainty and a strong need for acceptance and self-promotion. These are negative qualities that a great leader always avoids because of the message they send, which is the very opposite of what he or she wishes to project: confidence, assuredness and strong character.

Remember the old adage: "You are how you are perceived". And never be afraid to change your position. It may be that you were ignorant of the true nature of things. We all learn with time, experience and new knowledge. One does not wish to be seen as rigid, merely because change is uncomfortable and even more uncomfortable to state. Sometimes change is necessary to get back on track and to meet the changing circumstances around achievement of an objective. Being defensive about it is self-defeating and makes the leader look 'small'.

A leader is in a unique position. A leader's response and attitude say much about that leader. In addition, folks may not be able to articulate what they don't like when seeing such pettiness but they respond negatively, nonetheless. Folks look to a leader to 'lead', so that a negative perception of any kind, such as 'pettiness, 'self-defensiveness ' and 'thin skinnedness', should be avoided.

Part 1: Characteristics of a Good, Effective Leader

Smile: Friendliness Goes a Long Way

What does a smile cost? Nothing at all. No need to appear too 'serious' or even 'unfriendly'. You do not want to appear 'off-putting', as if any interruption is a bothersome nuisance.

This is true whether one deals with technical development projects or general sales. The effect is still the same. Customers feel most at ease when the interface is friendly, informative and welcoming. Staff feel likewise.

Smiling and an accomodating manner go a long way towards setting a customer at ease and towards capturing eventual sales. Even if the customer does not buy at that instant, a customer will return if the exchange is friendly, helpful, and comfortable. The benefit may not appear immediately, but may still bear fruit at some later time when the customer eventually returns. The key is in developing 'relationships' with the potential customer, without any sales pressure. The rewards may come later and take longer to mature but the rewards are usually more permanent, and consistent.

Staff feels most motivated when task requests are accompanied by a friendly smile. Under such circumstances, the staff will usually 'go the extra mile' to please and to accomodate the requestor.

So a leader will recognize this long term pay-off with his or her customer, and may even interface in a similar way with his or her own staff. That is not to say that a leader should tolerate insubordination, or disrespect either. There needs to be a fine balance between 'friendliness 'and 'respect'. Remember: 'It is always better to be feared and respected than to be loved'. Even one who 'loves' another can be disrespectful and abusive, at times. Never allow this to happen. Remember, a leader is always 'on stage'. Others are constantly watching and assessing a leader.

I have stated an old adage above. It is certainly true when given only two choices. However, this can be a false choice between only two alternatives. There is indeed a third choice: be both friendly <u>and</u> respected. There are times to be firm, commanding and demanding respect. There are other times when it is best to be friendly. One need not negate the other.

As a former PM, I'd often have to walk over to other buildings for various purposes. I'd seek out various individuals, and I'd chat with them for about 5 or 10 minutes...just enough to be friendly. By doing so, I was building relationships...bonding, if you will. When the time came, often many months later, I knew I could count on some of these same folks to pull me through a temporary bind. I would often get support through a harassing weekend, when no other manager could get the same level of support. Why? Because they wanted to help out a 'friend'. It was no longer just business. This happened often and it allowed us to see each other as work friends, not just as business co-workers.

The morale: Try to build relationships with your staff, with your customers, with others in your workplace that you don't often call upon for help. I found that very few leaders did this. It was my 'secret' weapon. I am sharing this now but I kept this method to myself for many years. As a result, I could often count on others to do what they'd never do for others because I took the time, when I expected nothing in return, to show that I cared about their day, their problems, their families, their daily challenges...and I genuinely did.

Part 1: Characteristics of a Good, Effective Leader

We both shared our humanity in the process, and when 'push came to shove', I found I really did not have to insist. The offer usually came voluntarily. They were helping 'me' out, personally - not just another PM or leader. That was the main difference. Their allegiance was to me personally, not to my position. Try it. The investment is often well worth it! It may mean the difference between success and failure. In the process, you will be sharing your 'humanness', as stated earlier. You will become a better, more approachable human being, as well as a better leader.

My demonstration of genuine caring payed off big time. I shared some personal confidences with them, although not excessively so. This showed the recipient that I trusted them as much as they were trusting me. It was mutual and it went both ways. Allowing another to share their confidences without a reciprocal sharing often doesn't work because the trust is only one-way, not two-way, as it ought to be.

When I finally retired in 2007, about 65 people attended the announcement of my Retirement. The two VP's that I reported to said some good words and some honest words about me that caused the audience to break out in laughter. My integrity and honesty, at any and all costs, was recognized by many in the audience and so they laughed when this 'foible' was stated by the senior VP. The audience consisted mostly of folks from Software and Hardware Engineering, Project Management, Systems Engineering, Assembly, Manufacturing, Accounts Receivable and Payable, Time-keeping, Publications, Quality Assurance, Quality Engineering, Document Control, and various levels of management, etc. In other words most departments of the company were represented there because of my 5-minute interaction with so many of them. Yet, they had been my unseen support through some very tough assignments.

Try to be friendly. Smile...it costs you nothing and yet it may reap many unexpected benefits. Meanwhile be sure to earn everyone's respect at the same time. This is rarely taught academically in school. Yet, in a very practical sense it can really make a difference in development, in achieving difficult corporate goals, or even in generating more sales. A customer will return if he or she is treated in a friendly yet helpful manner. He or she may not otherwise.

In addition, if this same principle is applied to one's staff, chances are they too will see this as positive, as long as the proper respect is also demonstrated, both ways, and the staff will extend itself to accomodate the wishes of the leader.

If you wish to be treated with respect, you must do the same with others... even with reports and customers.

If you come across a customer or staff member who is uninformed, do not become opinionated and shut down. Instead, do your very best to educate that individual, but be sure to do it in a non-condescending or non-patronizing manner, so that the individual does not become defensive or alienated. If a customer, he or she may wish to leave...never to return because of negative treatment due to an unguarded comment. If a staff member, suppressed anger and frustration may be the result, when the leader throws his or her weight around, especially in an unfriendly and disrespectful manner.

Try to say everything with a friendly tone and a genuine smile, if possible. Such an approach can be very disarming and very productive. You will not be sorry with the long-term results.

Part 1: Characteristics of a Good, Effective Leader

Recognize Performance Even if You Have to Pay for it Yourself

It is most necessary to recognize excellent performance. This cannot be said enough times. It is that important!

Sometimes this excellence is performed by one or a few employees. Sometimes it is the entire team. In either case, recognition and positive verbal feedback is needed. It helps to build positive team morale. Team members usually wish to excel. Acknowledging such superlative performance sends a positive message back to all team members that excellent performance is recognized by the leader. It helps to encourage further excellent perfomance by the recognized individual (s) and by the entire team too.

During my career as a leader, I'd make sure that this rule was always followed. The feedback could take various forms: quarterly recognition awards, generous salary increases, write-ups in the company paper, special luncheons, 'pats on the back', verbal recognition at meetings identifying the excellent performer, bonuses, etc.

At Christmas time I'd always buy, out of my own pocket, a bottle of wine or chocolates for each team or staff member. It was important for them to see that their efforts were being recognized and appreciated. It was one small thing, among many, that relayed this message.

The last company I worked for gave a Christmas and a birthday gift. At Christmas time, they also hosted an employees-only Christmas fiesta, during work hours, which was separate from the annual company-wide Christmas

Dinner, wherein spouses and other halves were invited to attend. Small tokens, but effective nonetheless.

It was a wonderful company to work for because the company always appreciated and went out of its way to demonstrate that it appreciated the efforts of its staff. The staff knew it and one could always hear how they perceived the company...very positively. That is the pay back. The company's extended efforts did not fall blindly. Instead, it raised morale to the point where no one ever wanted to leave the company, except for relocation, or some dire circumstance.

A little recognition and appreciation can go a very long way. It is often not the magnitude of the recognition itself, but the fact that management and the leadership recognizes their efforts, acknowledges them and appreciates them, even with some very small, even minute, tokens of appreciation.

Doing so gives back a whole lot more than it costs to pay for the small token. Rarely does the cost or the magnitude become a factor. Rather the required time and thoughtfulness garners the positive response from the team.

Give it a try. I believe that you will find that it has the potential of becoming a force multiplier with your team. They will know how much their efforts are recognized and appreciated. It cannot hurt to try and the benefits often outweigh the investment. Every good and effective leader realizes this simple fact. Without a motivated team there is no point in even trying, but with one the results can be phenomenal. Remember: 'The whole can be greater than the sum of its parts', if led and if managed properly! That is the true role of the leader, to tap into that fountain and to develop it, beyond the mundane expectations of others who are not so enlightened.

Part 1: Characteristics of a Good, Effective Leader

Delegation & Empowerment

A leader must delegate. If he or she does not delegate, then something is wrong and success will never be achieved. Delegation allows the leader to pursue other higher priority tasks. It also allows the assigned individual to 'prove himself or herself'. Delegation shows the leader's confidence in the ability of the assignee to do the required job.

However, with delegation of authority comes responsibility and accountability...especially in task management and other 'leadership' positions where one is responsible for the output of others, and not just oneself. There is a strong need to not only hold one accountable but to follow through with decisive actions as a result of that accountability, when necessary. This can be positive in terms of financial or social rewards for exemplary performance and achievement.

It can also be corrective, by replacing the unsuccessful assignee with another, by negative performance reviews, etc. This may only be necessary when the assigned individual is not performing as expected. Upbraiding an assignee in 'public' for all to see is never a 'good' idea. If necesssary, take the individual aside, and speak frankly but privately. Also, never forget to first tell the individual all that he or she is doing well. Then talk about areas of needed improvement. This prevents alienation of the very employee that you are trying to inspire. Besides, alienation by that individual can cause a depression in team morale if not handled correctly, and the assignee becomes demoralized and spreads his or her alienation around for all to see. Team morale can plummet in such circumstances.

A leader should try to create the circumstances for every team member to succeed. It is also very important to provide the resources necessary for the desired success. No individual can succeed if the necessary resources are denied, no matter how capable or talented.

Likewise, a 'leader' seeks to 'empower' his staff. This means no micromanagement, except on very rare occasions (see previous discussion, elsewhere in this book). This means pushing authority (and responsibility) to the lowest possible level. Doing so 'empowers ' the team and great results can occur consequently.

One must always be mindful that delegation and empowerment, must always be monitored and feedback provided, or else there is no way of knowing that either is successful, in a timely manner. If the wrong individual has been assigned to do a task, and that individual is failing miserably. This must be identified and corrected immediately by the leader. The 'leader' does not wish to discover this as the project schedule is near the end, because there will be no time, and most likely no funds left to take timely corrective action, to save the project or achieve the team goal. At that point correction is too little, too late.

Delegation and empowerment are essential. They allow inclusion of the team staff members in the overall success of the project or goal. A leader should never overlook this reality.

Part 1: Characteristics of a Good, Effective Leader

Unity, Not Devisiveness

A true 'leader' never tries to be devisive. Instead, he or she ought to strive for unity of purpose. Why? Because devisiveness is negative and non-constructive. It causes individuals to become defensive and to find someone or something to blame. It causes a similar division of resources and it defeats the principle stated earlier, 'that the whole is greater than the sum of its parts'. Instead of staff members working together in synergy, towards a common goal, there will be a great deal of infighting, defensiveness, self-protection, reduced, constructive risk-taking and finger-pointing. All this is very undesirable and very negative.

Unifying the team is the 'leader's' task. He or she sets the project tone, through his or her own communicated expectations, behavior and attitude. The leader does not stoke the fires of strife. Instead, the leader tries to encourage cooperation and tolerance. He or she encourages a stated 'difference of opinion'. Knowledge or information is gained from becoming aware of new and different approaches...not from trying the same tired old thing. Therefore diversity of opinion ought to be respected and encouraged, as long as it is stated respectfully.

It is much better to deal with an issue 'head-on' and quickly, than to let it remain unattended and fester. Such prompt action helps to build unity. Unity is just what it says: 'One' with a common goal or 'united' in achieving that same goal. A single purpose (that of the project or task) is what is meant here. There are no two purposes, only one, that is to say, the success of the overall project or assignment.

Divisiveness will not get you there. Following the analogy of magnetic dipoles: magnets get their strength because the small magnetic dipoles within it align themselves with each other, and thereby reinforce each other. Hence, their magnetic fields also align magnifying the total magnetic effect. They all face the same direction.

Much the same is true of Unity vs Devisivenes. Unity is analogous to magnetic dipole alignment and it produces a large overall positive effect, where as devisiveness is analogous to the random non-alignment of dipoles in a non-magnetized sample. In the last case, there is no alignment, Instead, there is a random distribution of dipole orientations and a generally weakened magnetic situation. The same can be said of a leader's team. All members must be aligned and working towards the same end goals.

The 'leader' always wants his staff to be working in a state of 'unity' because it creates the greatest harmony among staff members, the greatest synergy and the magnification of the efforts of each individual. On the other hand, devisiveness will produce the very opposite, negative result with each individual's contribution remaining individual and not helping to magnify the total effect.

Given that the 'leader' and all concerned staff members wish to share in the overall success of the project or assignment, chances are that this is not achievable without the necessary "unity' of purpose in the team. Devisiveness will most likely not allow success to be attained.

The conclusion: Unity is always superior in terms of the attainment of positive results than is devisiveness. Remember the old, but true adage: "United we stand, divided we fall."

Part Two:

Specific

Techniques

for Leaders

Part 2: Specific Techniques for Leaders

The Importance of Planning

Planning for any leader is essential. It can make the difference between success and failure. Planning at the highest level can be accomplished by the leader. The leader is always responsibile for obtaining the plan and for its proper execution. This is to ensure that the company or project objectives are met or exceeded. Company sales projections are often based upon the successful execution of such plans.

However, for the best results, it makes good sense to consult with your team leaders and the team, so that there is 'buy-in' by them. This is necessary because, the team must feel 'ownership' of the plan and therefore must contribute to the plan's formulation and execution. Without some kind of 'ownership' there is no way that success can be achieved. A plan developed without their considered input is doomed to failure, because the team/staff have not made any committment to it, i.e. they don't 'own' it. As a result, they feel no need to extend themselves to achieve what has been promised by another. They had no part in its formulation. The plan may therefore be completely unrealistic and unachievable.

Not only that, the team may feel that their input is unworthy or is not being considered by the leader. An unconsulted 'plan' may just be a mere 'fantasy', incapable of achievement. Instead, the team must feel that the plan is achievable and 'do-able'. They must believe in the plan. That can only happen when they have had a significant part in deriving the inputs for the plan. Only then will they marshall around the mutually-derived plan and work towards its realization. A motivated team will then work extra hours to ensure that their own contribution is successful and timely. In that way, they know that they are contributing to the success of the plan that they helped devise. Everyone wants to succeed, especially when they have made their own commitment towards that success.

To be truly realistic and attainable, input should flow from the workers to the managers or leaders. Only then can a plan be realistic and attainable. This is true whether the effort is a technical development project or a sales effort. The same rule applies either way. Sales projections can certainly be reviewed and revised by the leader based upon his or her experience, but no 'buy-in' will occur if the team is excluded from the process.

If the plan is developed only by the leader it sends the wrong message: the team's input has not been considered either because the 'leader' has no faith in his or her own team, or the leader doesn't care because he or she sees himself or herself as 'all knowing' and arrogant. This alienates the very staff that is essential to achieving the project goals. This is very undesirable, and smacks of arrogance and 'micro-management', a no-no.

The key, for any leader, is flexibility and a sense of nimbleness...the ability to seize fortune when it arises and so exploit the unexpected opportunity to the advantage of the team and the project. A 'good' leader realizes that any project is dynamic...not static. To achieve success, the leader and the team must also be dynamic and willing to change if the need or the opportunity arises. There is no room for 'dogma' or 'doctrine' in running a project. Instead, a leader must demonstrate adaptability and flexibility. The team will quickly recognize these qualities as essential in a true 'leader'. He or she must become totally 'pragmatic', if there is to be any chance of success.

Part 2: Specific Techniques for Leaders

In the case of Retail, a leader must be familiar with the company stock of items and their location. Otherwise, the leader or the team can miss sales opportunities. The leader must be seen as knowledgeable about company policies and procedures also, so that when a team member asks a question a knowledgeable answer can be provided. Otherwise, confidence in the knowledgeability of the leader comes into question. The same holds true for knowledge of the company's computer and tracking systems.

A 'pro' in managing a technical team is to be aware, in detail, of the technical requirements of a project. Oftentimes, the requirements or specifications of a development project are not even totally understood by the customer. I had this happen to me. I once had to manage a Fixed Price Contract and to produce four receiver and collection systems. However, I quickly realized that one of the specifications made no sense, given the application we had to support in the field. I found that one specification had been lifted 'word-for-word' out of a specification produced by the ASAE (American Society of Automotive Engineers). Whoever had written the specification lifted it 'verbatum' out of this document, without any real consideration as to whether it was really applicable or necessary for this particular application. It turned out that the specification was not applicable to our current development. I called the customer and related this concern to him. Within one week, this specification was eliminated from the requirements. This saved a considerable amount of cost and risk to the fixed price contract. It's elimination guaranteed the financial, technical and schedule success of the fixed price contract. Again some replanning became necessary but the incident presented an unexpected opportunity to succeed and so we grabbed this opportunity. The program was so successful, in every sense, that the customer wrote a letter of commendation to the CEO of the company I worked for.

I have presented this last example, not to brag, but instead to highlight the need for the leader to always be vigilant, questioning and flexible. It can make all the difference in the world. Imagine too the esteem it brings to the leader when the leader is seen by the team as ever-vigilant and flexible!

Part 2: Specific Techniques for Leaders

Organizing For Success

Here, I plan to discuss "Organizing For Success". It sounds almost straight forward and simple, but, believe it or not, this simple technique, once implemented properly can result in unforeseen efficiences and ultimate project success. Furthermore, it is truly amazing how many PM's and department managers overlook this powerful tool!

I was once approached by a company Founder to run a project that was well-nigh impossible to achieve. Being unbashful, I told him so. He wanted me to run a project that required development of a system, hardware and software development, without a specification, without a contract, accommodate a laboratory and office move from one building to another...all in 3 months. It normally required 18 months to develop a new system of this type, without these caveats and with a known and defined system specification. Three months alone were normally required to acquire parts and materials, once the design, development and subsystem & system tests and documentation were in place. It was a terribly aggressive challenge. The Founder came to me because I had turned around projects before and I, with good technical teams, had saved several projects and achieved success with others, which had many difficulties and challenges.

As a matter of fact, I told him it was "impossible to achieve, given the many constraints", but I still kept an open mind.

I spent the entire night thinking and scheming how it might be achieved, in spite of my many misgivings. I have always been very patriotic, and I wanted so much to make this work, impossible as it first seemed. I quickly realized that the critical key was 'organization'. I would have an excellent technical team, but that in itself did not guarantee success. I needed something much more!

The very next morning I came into work, tired from a lack of sleep, but motivated nonetheless. I then set about setting up an organizational structure that would give us a chance...not a guarantee, as I then told the Founder and the prospective government customer.

I then sought out a very capable technical system engineer. I spoke to him in 'no uncertain terms'. Even my own V. P. boss could not get him to perform, as desired. The V. P. saw him as unproductive at best! I felt that he was a valuable resource that had not been approached or motivated properly. I approached him with brutal honesty. Yet, I also told him of his many positive contributions on other tasks. Given the proper direction, I felt he was very capable of great things. I gave him full authority and responsibility for the technical success of the project, while I set up half-hour daily action item (AI) meetings with the technical staff, and bi-daily meetings with the materials and parts procurement staff, which would obtain and track the acquisition of parts, metal fabrication and other materials.

I established accountable task leaders, who owed me their allegiance and who were held accountable for the responsibilities and authority they were assigned. I informed the government customer weekly about our progress, while telling him that I could not guarantee success itself, but I could guarantee that we'd do everything possible to meet the aggressive goal. I also told him that 'if the equipment is ready in 3 months and sitting on the shipping dock, it would remain there until a contract was finally awarded.' Up to that point, we had been funded via company internal funds only. That entire three-month period, the team and I worked incessantly. Through that "summer of Hell", as we termed it, we often worked weekends and did development upgrades at 3 am to meet the needs of the project. As it turned out, the government took 3 months to write the contract, while we took that same 3 months to develop, build and test an entirely new system...all with a very untimely lab. move to another building and no system specification from the customer. The customer finally came through with a signed contract on the same day the system was to be delivered, on time to the shipping dock.

Organization was the key to success.

On another occasion, I told my brother-in-law how to organize for a new position he had undertaken at a gun-manufacturing company. I told him that he could not be successful, with a dozen or so direct reports. I instead suggested that he hire a couple of supervisors, who would be loyal to him (since he hired them and did their performance reviews).

These supervisors would monitor and direct the day-to-day affairs, but he was to hold them accountable for the authority and responsibility he granted them. That would free him to look at the 'big picture' and to make any needed modifications, as necessary. He did implement my recommendations and he was quite successful in his new career move.

This same emphasis on organization can bear positive results in a sales or retail company. Proper organization can allow the proper flow of work and the dissemination of critical information. It can motivate the sales or retail team and bring focus to their activities. They will know who to ask if there is an issue that requires prompt resolution.

In summary, organization can make a world of

difference in the likely success of a particular project. Don't overlook this important aspect, if you wish your project or assignment to be successful.

Part 2: Specific Techniques for Leaders

Team Building: Another Element in Project Success

Often overlooked as a factor in successful project completion is the need to build a strong, loyal, effective team. Without a 'good' team, the best leader in the world cannot achieve his or her project goals. They are interdependent for true success to occur. A positive outcome is unattainable without both a good leader and a good team. They 'go hand in hand'. Each drives the other towards successful achievement of the end goals. Not only must the team be effective and capable, it must be loyal to the leader and share in the leader's own end goals for the project.

Without the loyalty, dedication and commitment of the team, there will be no 'force multiplier', no leveraging of resources (staff and others) and the synergies that might otherwise arise are not within reach. With a positive, effective, loyal and committed team, anything is possible! It results in the 'whole (team) being greater than the sum of its parts (individual contributions)' Ultimately, that is the very point in developing teams or team spirit. It allows the team and the leader acting in concert, to achieve great things. Now that we have highlighted why it is important to develop teams, the obvious question that soon arises is: And how does one develop a team?

Amazingly enough, it does not require very much. It all comes back to the leader having a genuine concern for the welfare and the morale of his or her team. Once that threshold of concern is crossed the rest is easy!

Team building comes about by creating an 'esprit de corps', as in the military. Once 'team spirit' is developed, staff will often sacrifice themselves or their personal time to ensure the overall success of the project. I have seen this many times. Many folks wish to be part of something greater than themselves. It gives them real goals to achieve. With achievement, through selfless acts, or through helping one another, greater progress can be made. Associated with that comes a great sense of achievement.

'Team Spirit' can be built by a variety of methods. There really is no right way or wrong way. Do whatever it takes to build allegiance and to facilitate achievement. Ensure that outstanding performance is recognized and demonstrated to other team members with awards, prizes, etc.

Award quarterly financial awards for great performance. Use the company newspaper to build pride in the team's achievements with photos and relevant articles. Give high salary increases to outstanding performers. Advertise their achievements as models for others to follow. (This has been mentioned before, but it requires repeating because it is so important.) Have group luncheons, recognize birthdays among team members, have special events (bowling, golf, touch football, etc.).

I found that creating tee shirts with project logos or even coffee mugs with the same was very effective. Create financial or gift incentives for achieving important project milestones. Ensure continued committment by granting bonuses and announce them. Don't be afraid to set realistic but difficult challenges. You might be surprised at the positive responses, given 'real' leadership. Good performers delight in achieving difficult goals. It builds their confidence and makes them feel worthy...and proud of their accomplishments. This should be encouraged by the leader.

Distribute photographs of the project team, systems

or products. Frame them and overlay them with signed plastic to individualize and personalize them. It is amazing what simple actions such as these can have on team performance. I have instituted many of these ideas myself, with received benefits that are much greater than the immediate cost outlay.

The strange thing is that some of these actions have a retention or spill-over effect. If a team sees that it is visibly recognized for its efforts or if, in other words, the leader appreciates their efforts, the word will get around and talented staff will want to work for that sensitive but strong leader on some very difficult assignments. Hence, not only will the immediate project benefit but the effect may very well 'spill over' into future projects. Team staff and its leader will both become recognized as being extraordinary. Talented individuals will embrace the opportunity to work with a leader who appreciates their extraordinary efforts. Most talented individuals are motivated by difficult challenges... not intimidated. The end result is usually always positive and successful. Give it a try!!

So, what can derail such attempts? Answer: lack of accountability and follow-thru. As said before, a leader is 'always on stage'. His or her actions are always visible, eventually, to the team. So, be careful with what you are seen to do, not just what you say. If they don't match it will eventually be noticed by the team and all trust in the leader will quickly vanish. Also, with leadership, management, etc., comes responsibility and authority. However, it also comes with accountability. One ought to be held accountable for non-achievement, chastised privately, corrective action taken and seen, and/or have the staff member replaced with someone more effective. If this is not done then the truly effective workers will become demoralized, realizing that one's performance does not matter, because there is no accountability. It can be like a cancer, eating away at the host. All one's efforts to build a 'team' will disappear quickly if there is no accountability shown evenly and fairly, and at all levels.

More junior staff members, who have not yet obtained the necessary experience or exposure, often overlook various procedures or they are wildly optimistic about what it takes to achieve certain results. Such staff members are often reluctant to admit difficulty in solving a problem, that other more senior staff members may have already encountered and resolved. The answer, in that case, is to remind that individual that the project is a 'team' effort and that he or she should never be embarrassed to ask for help or assistance, or even advice. Other team members are usually more than happy to render such assistance. Remember: 'the whole can be greater than the sum of its parts' only if the proper attention is given by the leader to foster such 'team work'.

Build one's team, as above, to increase chances of success. Give other team members an opportunity to achieve great things and to be part of something 'bigger than themselves' but be sure to hold everyone, at all levels, accountable. Without such 'follow-thru', other attempts at 'team building' will ultimately fail.

Part 2: Specific Techniques for Leaders

Team Building Continued: The 'Special' Sauce

Here, in this chapter, we continue the discussion of 'team-building'. It is very important and it needs extra emphasisbeceuse without a 'team' ther is little chance of achieving the established goals, whether they be project , slaes or corporate goals.

It sounds simple enough, and yet it is often missed as a key element in a project's or a leader's success or failure. For true success to occur, the path to that final success must be paved by the leader AND a diligent, competent team whose allegiance lies with the leader. So how does one accomplish this? The simple truth is that "team building" is the "secret or special" sauce in any successful venture!

The leader must first be totally aware that success depends upon a certain symbiosis between the team leader and the team itself. The leader must be honest, frank and forthright. Integrity is very important in building trust. Without experience and competence, the team will soon discover 'a lack of what is needed'. However, to truly succeed, the leader must not only incorporate these characteristics.

He or she must also be "realistic". Either too much optimism or too much pessimism are judged as unrealistic. Astute, experienced team members will easily see this. Hence, the result will be a loss in team 'drive' and 'enthusiasm' under that self-proclaimed 'leader'. I have found that there must be 'mutual respect' between team members and the team leader. Exchanges need to be fairly transparent to build trust and confidence. I also found through many years of experience one way to build trust is NOT to lay down arbitrary commands. A 'true' leader listens to good counsel. He (or she) is experienced enough and he (or she) is confident enough to hear the stated judgment of others, without recoiling defensively or in playing the loser's 'blame game'.

It really doesn't matter how one arrived where one finds oneself. What matters is what one is going to 'do' about the current situation? How do you plan to address the issue? In the corporate world there is no room for 'blame'. One is often chastised for playing that 'losing' game. The fault lies in the past and it is recognized that nothing can change what has already happened. In addition, 'blame' is a loser's game. The only relevant issue is; What is the currently asssigned team and its leader going to do NOW to fix the issue and to stop the bleeding? Anything else is considered a waste of time and resources and it may even cause alienation of previous teams. This is considered very undesirable.

Another thing I found to be revealing and instrumental in building team spirit, is to never ask one's team to do what the leader is unwilling to do himself or herself. It really comes down to 'management by example'. One reason that the German General Erwin Rommel was so popular with his troops in WW2, was his willingness to do what he asked others to do. In WW1, when he commanded his men to cross a freezing cold river in the midst of winter, Rommel was the first to set the example. He jumped into the river first. As a result of this action and others, his soldiers would have done anything he asked them.

Over time, his reputation carried him forward. The German troops under his command knew that he had their backs and their best interests in mind.

In the corporate or government world this means not asking staff to come in on a weekend or somehow work extra hours to catch up, which can be illegal on government

Part 2: Specific Techniques for Leaders

contracts. Never ask your team to do anything that you are not willing to do yourself. Volunteering of one's time is paramount. Building team spirit often results in such voluntary action, because the end result, success, is foremost in the team member's mind.

Team members will respect a leader who also sacrifices his own weekend for the project's well-being. The team needs 'to see' that the team leader is also willing to take on personal sacrifices. The result is increased respect for the leader.

When I was a project manager or even a Director, I would indicate to the tasked team member where we stood on a particular effort. I would show where we ought to be per the plan without doing anything further, and then I waited for the staff member to volunteer a solution. Volunteering was okay; it was not mandatory...nor should it be!

If they voluntarily came in on a weekend, I made sure that I too was visible. I also brought in donuts in the morning, or I brought in sandwiches or a pizza, etc. for lunch. Team members appreciated these relatively small gestures, and I found that it helped to build team spirit. It became quite clear that we (as a team) were all in this together, and we were all working together to achieve some very difficult goals. We would 'sink or swim' together.

Another thing that can cement teams together, so that the "whole is greater than the sum of the disparate parts" is by obtaining some personal momentos, that build 'esprit de corps' among the team members. Team members usually display these momentos very proudly.

Most of us wish to be treated with respect and consideration. If that is your guiding principle, it will quickly be recognized that the motivated and aligned team can create a 'win-win' outcome for all involved. 'Unthought of' synergies will naturally develop with the total effect of enhancing project or team performance. It will quickly become apparent that the team and the leader each need the other for ultimate success.

In summary, team building is essential to the success of any task or project. It provides leverage. It is a 'force multiplier'. Why not look at your team and determine if enough of this very important ingredient is present or missing, as you try to achieve success on your task or project.

Part 2: Specific Techniques for Leaders

Management By Walking Around (MBWA)

Most management and leadership occurs on a daily basis. The remainder usually occurs at weekly meetings. However, there is another way to determine what the status is for various tasks. It is often referred to as Management By Walking Around (MBWA). It can be very effective if done properly.

For example, if a project or asignment is particularly fast moving it may not make sense to wait until the weekly meeting comes around to take action. However, by walking around the hallways and work areas, the PM or leader can sometimes learn of things that are happening that the assigned person may be too embarrassed or uncomfortable exposing in a group setting (the old CYA syndrome).

This method is also useful for general management because it allows the manager or leader to see what is happening at that moment. It allows a very immediate level of feedback and control, provided that the findings and any new direction are somehow communicated promptly to the team at large, if they are affected. If sales stations are not properly or adequately staffed, theft is skyrocketing, there is insufficient stock, or if resources of any needed kind are in short order, interpersonnal issues exist, staffing issues exist, the premises are unclean, etc., these problems can quickly become apparent to the leaders merely by implementation of MBWA. The leader can assess whether certain areas require renewed attention, or an entirely new approach. It is very difficult to assess behind the manager's or leader's desk.

The daily interaction is missing. This can only be achieved by physically implanting oneself in the situation at hand or by outside observation. It allows instantaneous action or correction. It minimizes lost or incorrectly assigned time and effort.

The potential downfall in the MBWA methodology is that the encountered individual is being sampled at a time that is different from the other team members. Because of this, decisions made or information gathered may be different from what others have been told or understand, at a different time. Confusion and mixed signals can be the result of what appears to be a perfectly good way to obtain current information. This is especially true if one task depends upon another.

This can be corrected once again by proper and timely communication. This can be by means of a separate meeting, an e-mail message, a phone call, publication of a new directive, generation of a broadcast text message or some other means. This is especially true if other team members or the project itself is affected by the change in direction.

Given the caveats and the follow-through requirements above, I have found this method to be highly effective and timely. It allows for a fast reaction time.

Timely communication is the key. MBWA can be very effective, together with timely communication with other team members about any agreements or changes that were decided upon during MBWA.

With proper usage, this methodology can be very illuminating, allow timely correction, and improve overall performance. If done properly, it can be extremely effective.

Part 2: Specific Techniques for Leaders

Running Short But Effective Meetings

Here we discuss the real need to run effective but short meetings. Why is this important? I have seen many cases where a weekly meeting is held, regardless of need, and the meeting format is formless and therefore lasts much longer than it needs to, sometimes as long as 1.5 hours. The result: staff becomes bored, unmotivated and much less efficient in the performance of their responsibilities. It wastes the staff's time, when they could instead be making some real progress in achieving their assigned tasks. Further, if the meeting is scheduled in the middle of the afternoon, the unmotivated team will look upon the remainder of that half-day as a total loss, an occurrence no project or asignment can easily afford. In addition, if the meeting is held mid-week, then the same thing happens: lack of motivation together with a lost opportunity to set the work tone for the rest of the week, half of which has since past.

From many practical experiences, I have found that no matter how complex the task or project, no more than 30 - 45 minutes is needed for any meeting. All it takes is organization. pre-formatting, and discipline. In the case of the very aggressive three-month development, discussed earlier, many lessons were learned from that experience, especially concerning the running of efficient and very effective meetings.

Meetings should not be held, just for the sake of holding a meeting. If the meeting is not needed, redundant or unnecessary, cancel the meeting and free the staff to do what it does best.

An organized and efficient meeting shows the staff

that time is important and that the leader is aware of this. It also is an opportunity to show that the leader is organized and has his or her 'act together'.

If a development or assignment is extremely fast-paced then some hard-headed decisions need to be made and quickly. For one, the project must be organized in such a way as to allow for success.

There is an electrical law called Shannon's Law. Strangely, it found application in the management world. It states that in order to faithfully reconstruct a signal one has to know the bandwidth (fastest rate of change) of the signal and then it must be sampled at twice that bandwidth or change rate. Sounds awful technical doesn't it? However, I and my project team had once (discussed earlier) been given a high-rate of change assignment. It required a higher rate of monitoring and correction (AI's and more frequent, but short effective meetings) to pull it off. That is exactly what we did.

Individual recognition is essential to amplify the effect of any one person's contribution. We had regular special luncheons with recognition of outstanding performance. We worked 60 - 70 hours weekly for an entire summer. Sometimes we worked well into the wee hours of the morning. I rode critical programmable devices to Burlingame, CA from Sunnyvale, CA in my own vehicle to ensure safe and reliable air transport overseas. We also held very effective daily meetings that lasted 30 minutes and reviewed 250 action items, each day.

The key to effective meetings is indeed organization. We held these meetings every day until the goal was achieved. The Action Item (AI) List set the daily agenda and it was reviewed, new assignments made, priorities set and reset, assignees made with new or revised due dates. The AI 'Closed Items' were moved to the bottom of the list as

Part 2: Specific Techniques for Leaders

they were closed out. Over the three-month period, many, many AI's were closed out. The very few remaining AI's at the completion of the task, were very low priority and non-essential items, which were subsequently abandoned or ignored.

The organization centered around two main elements: establishing appropriately experienced task leaders and settting up a reporting system to collect current status, without unnecessarily overburdening the team staff. Much of this procedure has been discussed before and it will not be repeated here. An AI meeting was not held on Mondays, as on 'normal' development projects because it would have been redundant to the weekly meeting. Tight control and coordination were necessary to achieve a very aggressive schedule.

The staff, never spent any more than 2.5 hours per week (5 x 0.5 hrs) in meetings to achieve an extremely aggressive set of goals. A normal project should never require more than 30-40 minutes per week.

It is essential, that each staff person have an opportunity to voice his or her progress, problems or issues. Lengthy diatribes, on specific non-status items, may require separate meetings with only the interested persons attending. The key is to maintain a quick pace to allow the meeting to be short, effective and concise. Differing opinions should be allowed expression. The final decision rests, however, with the leader.

The weekly status reports stated milestone-oriented achievements, issues or problems, with proposed solutions or requests for management assistance and support. I recall one individual sent me a report that merely said that he or she was working on some task. I immediately sent it back as 'unacceptable'. After all, I had just assigned that person to the very task he was describing, so there was no exchange of information. "Tell me something I don't know and please answer in milestone terms only." That was my response. The follow-on report told me, in a milestone-oriented manner, what had or had not been achieved that week on the task. This was what was needed. It provided me with measurable progress on that specific task, not some ambiguous statement of 'progress' that was unmeasurable and subjective. I needed an objective measure, not a subjective one.

If the leader notices that some staff members are becoming sleepy, that is a clear indication that the meeting is much too long and needs to be shortened and made more effective. Don't be afraid to get feedback from the staff about meeting length and format. Such feedback is often insightful.

The weekly Status Review was milestone-oriented to ensure that progress was measurable (a milestone every one or two weeks apart), specifically with regard to completion of task milestones. I was most interested in what had been concretely and measurably achieved. The staff always knew what the meeting agenda was to be. Only senior people attended this weekly meeting. They, in turn, scheduled their own weekly meetings with their reports, so that comumunication was always achieved throughout the entire team.

...Communication, Comumunication, Communication!!

Each senior person spoke "round robin' about progress, problems and proposed solutions. If more detailed discussion was required, a separate meeting was scheduled on that topic, but only with the interested or affected personnel. It was a chance for all the senior task leaders to hear what was happening in other subtasks, to give credit for extraordinary achievement, and to solicit assistance in solving knotty problems. A normally scheduled monthly meeting was

Part 2: Specific Techniques for Leaders

held in which the entire general staff was briefed, so that all were equally informed about project status, milestone achievement, near term and long term goals, etc.

After any meeting's conclusion, I would usually publish Minutes of the Meeting to ensure a common understanding of what had been agreed to. The same held true for any other meetings in which decisions or changes in goals were agreed upon. Every 'team'/'staff' member was given the opportunity to read, review and comment on the published Minutes to ensure complete and full agreemenet. If necessary, the Minutes were republished with any necessary corrections. However, this never happened.

I organized the project team under a senior system engineer's authority. I gave him the wide technical authority he needed to succeed and I held him personally accountable for technical performance. He and the technical team did an outstanding job!

'Empower your staff'. Don't try to tell them how to do their own jobs. They know best what they are doing and they should be respected for that understanding and knowledge.

On the three-month project, I held <u>separate</u> meetings on Mondays, Wednesdays and Fridays with the Materials and Fab. Acquisiton Team to coordinate procurement of parts. Again an AI List was separately derived to drive this activity. I even called the VP of Manufacturing at a separate commercial Silicon Valley IC Fab facility to get special treatment and delivery of new parts. It all came down to discipline and organization...but in the end it resulted in project success and mission success!

By doing much of what is stated above, the project team remained alert, and focussed. We designed, built and delivered the system exactly within the 3 months required...

Thoughts On Leadership

and with a government contract in place. Everyone knew what was expected of him or her. As Project Manager and leader, I provided the necessary focus and organization to ensure success.

If the 'leader' is holding weekly meetings without an agenda and without an AI (Action Item) List, and if the normal weekly meeting lasts more than 45 minutes, the 'leader' needs to re-evaluate what the purpose of the meeting is and he/she needs to re-assess the effectiveness of these meetings and the resulting 'morale' or lack of it among of the project team, and then change as necessary.

Also, allow 10 minutes towards the end of the meeting for questions and answers, which will inevitably come, if the audience is awake and truly listening. If this period is becoming too lengthy, advise the questioner to see the speaker after the end of the meeting, so that others may return to work. Document the agreements and answers if necessary so that all know the result, not just the questioner.

It is amazing what can be accomplished when meetings are run effectively and efficiently. By so doing, the staff remains motivated and they are allowed more time to do their tasks. It reduces the project or assignment 'overhead', and focuses every member on what needs to be accomplished...not on reporting such progress, although this too is important. However, the time needed to report such progress ought to be kept to an absolute minimum.

Part 2: Specific Techniques for Leaders

E-Mail Saturation & How to Survive It

Most of us feel inundated, both at home and at work with mail: e-mail, phone mail, text messages, tweets, physical mail. It can easily be overwhelming. Worse than that it can leave one feeling enslaved to technology and its incessant demands. The solution: self-discipline. It is totally unnecessary to always feel 'connected'. That is a 'modern' phenomenon only. Hence, it can easily be dispensed with. 'Connection' is only useful if it results in increased productivity. If not, then it ought to be dispensed with, because it is then only another 'time-waster'.

One has to decide from the onset, whether one is to be technology's Master or its Slave. To put it differently, one has to decide whether it will be a Blessing or a Curse. The decision-maker: You and only You! The decision criteria ought to be either: consequence or potential productivity increase. Nothing else matters.

Here, I will only discuss e-mail. Many of the simple un-cluttering principles described here can be applied to any technology mentioned above. Further, these methods can also be applied at home, as well as at work.

Any good manager or leader realizes that the use of one's time is of paramount importance. It affects one's efficiency or productivity. Lots of time can and often is wasted because an individual blames the technology, instead of himself or herself. It really comes down to a recognition of the value of one's time.

Research has shown that 28% of a 'knowledge' (office) worker's time is spent dealing with e-mail. Imagine how much time one has left in a 40 hour week to do real 'work', when one includes phone responses, tweet responses, and others. It is conservative to estimate that at least a total of one half of a regular 40 hour work week is wasted on such items.

I have personally encountered this problem, in my career and at home. However, there is 'hope' as long as one is willing to exercise 'self-discipline'. Ask yourself: Do I really have to respond right now to the 'urgent' message? Is the message 'urgent' to someone else's needs or yours? Why not ignore or postpone? Is it really that 'important' or are you afraid of offending someone because of a failure to give a timely response? How is this affecting your accomplishment of your own 'needs' and 'requirements'? What is the 'consequence' of a delayed response? Will this help me be more productive? etc.

Here is a list of things to try:
1. Put your own 'needs' first, not someone else's.
2. Learn to say 'No' and to get yourself and others used to hearing it.
3. Scan all your messages before taking any action
4. First, delete any 'meaningless', or inconsequential messages.
5. Prioritize your messages. Some are high priority; others are low priority. Sort them accordingly.
6. Only answer 'urgent' or 'high priority' messages first. Postpone or do not answer 'low priority' messages.
7. Assign specific blocks of time to answer messages with the highest priority messages to be answered first.
8. Assign a short block of time three times a day: at early morning, when one first comes to work; at noontime or immediately after returning from lunch, for new high

Part 2: Specific Techniques for Leaders

priority messages and for old 'medium priority' messages; at the work day's end for the new high priority messages and for old 'medium or low priority' messages.

9. Label messages or set up specific folders to organize messages to allow fast and easy retrieval.

10. Use the latest technology, where possible, such as 'smart phones' or Blackberries, etc., to respond in an efficient, productive and timely manner. Don't be intimidated by new technology. Instead, use it where it increases your efficiency and productivity. Embrace it. Else, avoid it, if it merely wastes time.

11. Do not get caught up in the social media 'requirements'. This can be another great 'time-waster', with no real productivity gain.

One last thing: keep 'high priority' responses to less than six sentences, if possible. Time wasted on unnecesarily lengthy reponses is time that could be better utilized elsewhere.

All of these actions may help to manage the technical onslaught of e-mail. Many of these techniques can be used elsewhere and for other 'time wasters'. Give them a try. You may even find a few of your own.

They may work for you, but remember the central key is: 'self-discipline. You do not have to answer every request. Learn to say 'No' when necessary for your own survival. If someone is using or abusing this technology to make incessant requests that only support that individual's need for status or information, perhaps it is then time to meet that person face-to-face to discuss the abuse and the fact that their demands are disallowing you from achieving your own goals or requirements.

Remember: It is up to YOU to establish the necessary

'boundaries' so that you can get done whatever is needed or required of you. Become your own master. Do not allow technology to enslave you. Technology can be a 'boon', if used properly and judiciously, It can be a productivity increaser, but it can also be a great time-waster, depending on its usage. The decider is you,

Part 2: Specific Techniques for Leaders

Stress Management

A leader's job, whether he or she is a line manager, a store manager, a Program or a Project Manager is highly stressful. Many, many crucial decisions need to be made each day. Unforeseen circumstances arise from many quarters: staffing, customers or other contractors (if the project is under a sub-contract with a larger contractor), situational events, facilities or assets, parts shortages, unavailable staff, security clearances, corporate management, etc. In fact, the list is almost endless. So the pressing question is: Why would one subject oneself to such a situation, and how does one manage the associated stress?

The answer to this question is fairly straightforward. There is a great satisfaction in solving great challenges and finding solutions to difficult problems. There is definitely a great deal of stress to deal with. So again, how does one manage a high level of stress?

There are very many books available that address this issue. I will only address a few that I have found helpful in my 38-year career.

There are some activities that may or may not help stress, or they may appear to help initially, although they may have long-term negative affects. I am talking about drinking multiple cups of coffee each day, especially with lots of sugar. The same is true of many soft-drinks. Many contain, not only sugar but lots of caffeine. I am not advocating doing this at all. As a matter of fact, I used to 'take some coffee with my sugar'. A very bad move indeed! I used to call it my 'go-go' juice for obvious reasons. There is only one caveat, such an approach may help in the short term, but bring about serious health issues in the longer term. (Same for Coke and other sugary soft drinks.) This was a 'bad' choice, but I have only come to realize it lately. Now, I consume no sugar at all with my green tea.

I did develop some good habits too for managing the high level of daily stress. For one thing, I learned to say 'no' so that I could control my time, not the other way around. I also learned to close my office door for a couple of hours each day to discourage entry and unnecessary interruptions or consumption of my time. In other words, I learned and practised some Time -Management techniques.

I would use my 'closed door' time to do pushups or other exercises, privately and unobtrusively. One could just as easily perform some yoga poses or meditational exercises, during this time period. Sometimes, I used this 'quality' time to do some pressing work requirements of my own. Either way, it helped to relieve the stress I was experiencing, on the inside.

I also found that deep slow breathing helped me to handle the stressful burdens of leadership. There was one other technique that I utilized often. Whenever, things were getting to me too much, I'd take long walks through the long building hallways, while breathing deeply and rhythmically. By the time I had returned to my office, my stress level had been reduced dramatically.

At lunch time, I'd often eat a lunch that I had brought from home to avoid eating unhealthy foods. I'd bring yogurt and a piece of fruit to eat. Then, instead of working through lunch, which was often very tempting, given my overloaded comittments, I'd take a 2 or 3 mile walk to relieve some stress. I highly recommend doing so.

Another thing is to avoid the need to buy and consume 'snack' items at the vending machines in the cafeteria area. Most of these, contain high levels of sugar, unhealthy fat and/or salt, none of which are good for you. They may satisfy a short-term need and even give you a short-term boost but that quickly fades. Meanwhile, you are undoing your health.

In summary, learning to relax and reduce stress requires conscious action. The stress itself can cause poor decision-making that may ultimately affect your health on a negative way. The effect may not be immediately obvious but may instead show up much later in life. So choose your stress-relief methods carefully and rationally... not impulsively. One must take positive control if one is to succeed in controlling stress. It doesn't just happen by itself, unless one is a very rare individual.

Every leader needs to control the ubiquitous stress. Otherwise, the team will become the target for irrational actions that are really a result of being overburdened, with no relief for the leader...and that is highly undesirable. It cuts into the team's perception of one as an effective leader, because one criteria of a great leader is the ability to never show or demonstrate stress. 'Never let 'em (the team or any one else) see you sweat!'

Appendices

Thoughts On Leadership

Appendix A: Work Breakdown Structures (WBS)

Appendix A:
Breaking Down a Project
Into Its Component Parts:
Work Breakdown Structure (WBS)

Ever wonder how a large contractor can estimate the development cost of a very large and very complex project or task? How does the contractor arrive at an estimate of the cost?

These are intriguing questions, and yet, as with most everything, it comes down to organization. In this case, it comes down to breaking each complex major task into its smaller, more manageable component parts or elements. After this is accomplished, the bidding to achieve each of the simpler component parts can be identified in a straightforward manner. This is where the Work Breakdown Structure (WBS) comes into play. It does exactly that. It defines all the component parts that are required to be completed, identifies them and organizes them within the WBS. To collect actual cost accruals later, once the contract is awarded, such a WBS is often used to help set up the labor charging structure and their associated task charge numbers.

To achieve the best accuracy, it is usually best to leave the bidding or estimation to the 'doers', with management oversight to account for lapses, or inexperience. In other words, let those who are most familiar with the types of tasks required do the bidding, with more experienced task leaders and senior staff reviewing the bids to account for excessive optimism on the part of the less experienced bidders. By involving the 'doers' in the estimation process, they feel a sense of involvment and of 'ownership' when and if the estimate is accepted by the customer and the contract to do the work is received. This alone can help to achieve project success.

If some of the bidders are inexperienced it is not uncommon for them to be unduly optimistic in their bids. This is why management review is necessary. These inexperienced but well-meaning individuals often assume 100% efficiency, which of course, never happens. There are meetings, phone mail and e-mail, coffee breaks, smoke breaks, hallway discussions, 'potty' breaks, unanticipated problems or issues, etc. All of these and more bring the actual efficiency closer to 50%, which is more realistic and ought to be reflected in the actual estimate, because it does reflect reality. Usually, experienced senior staff recognizes this discrepancy and makes the necessary estimate adjustments from such individuals.

In addition, there is usually a second review by upper management or the executive staff. Why is this needed? The executive staff is aware of staffing and business needs that may not be accounted for elsewhere. In a competitive environment, the executive staff may decide to underbid the project for competitive reasons or to ensure that the needed project is captured, to meet sales or revenue goals. However, such underbidding can present some issues once the execution phase of the effort is underway. At this point, the program or project manager is wisest who seeks ways to eliminate or reduce risk from the project and to set aside a small (10%) financial reserve that he or she can draw upon should the project run into trouble.

The use of a financial reserve is very similar to the use of military reserves by the Armed Services. One never truly knows in advance whether there will ever be a need

App. A: Work Breakdown Structures

to assign the Reserve, but it is certainly the prudent action to take. With a reserve, the resources can be applied to the needed area as required and at the appropriate time. It can mean the difference between 'success' and 'failure', if properly applied.

In summary, the WBS is a very important financial organizational structure that allows a contractor to reasonably estimate the effort to achieve the requirements of an RFP (Request For Proposal). The proposed WBS often becomes the starting point for the new development once the contract is awarded. However, the contract type (to be discussed in Apprndix C) is just as important to the contractor. The Executive may choose to override these concerns for business reasons. However, doing so often makes the project more difficult to achieve should the contract be awarded to the contractor.

Thoughts On Leadership

Appendix B: Earned Value Methods (EVM) For Large Projects

Appendix B: Earned Value Methods for Large Projects

Throughout this book, we have often alluded to the use of Earned Value Methods (EVM) to control and manage large projects. Oftentimes, for smaller projects, it is too costly and too labor intensive to try to implement such measures. However, the larger the project, the more desirable it is to implement EVM. Further, oftentimes the customer will require EVM on financially significant development projects. After all, they are paying for the risky development. They rightly want to know what they are getting and when, and whether the project is on track, schedule-wise, cost-wise and performance-wise...hence the contractual requirement often for EVM implementation, especially for cost-plus type contracts (please see Appendix C).

Many of these EVM methods were developed to control the complex development of the lunar/space program, via NASA. They not only had to deal with complex technical developments but they also had to control hundreds, perhaps thousands, of subcontractors. Schedule and cost monitoring alone were insufficient to guarantee success. Hence, these methods were defined and implemented. EVM allowed the government agencies to not only quantify cost and schedule, but also to measure accomplishments and progress against the 'plan'. It also allowed for a reasonable estimate of the working remaining to be done in the event of cost or schedule overruns.

EVM allows the measurement of achievement...not

just how much it is costing, or when it will be completed but it gives feedback on what is being accomplished or done. It illuminates what has been achieved, in terms of measurable milestones, or what remains to be done in similar terms.

The key to effective EVM is the breaking down of tasks into small enough WBS elements. What is small enough? Each task ought to contain several measurable milestone events, of about one to two weeks duration for each milestone. Each of these milestones can then be quantified as to duration and cost, depending upon the time required to do the task and the loaded labor rate(s) of the assignee(s).

If each milestone requires 6 man weeks to achieve in two weeks, and the subtask requires four such milestones, then the schedule is 8 weeks long, the cost is 24 manweeks times the cost per man-week for the entire subtask. Depending on the cost per man-week of the assigned personal, the task cost can and will vary. In the example above, the EVM 'planned' amount is as stated. What may change is the 'actual' realized EVM cost, once the effort is underway.

Let us assume that, at a particular point during the task, e.g. at the 4 week point, one had to assign a more senior person to the task. Not only would the subtask 'actual' cost increase, but if only 1 milestone would have been completed. Then, the subtask would cost more than originally estimated and only 1 milestone would have been achieved instead of 2. At this point, this subtask is clearly in trouble. There is not only a cost overrun for what has been achieved, the schedule has slipped and the measured 'actual' level of achievement is also much lower than expected, when the actual EVM is compared to the EVM plan.

A good leader would recognize this by evaluating both the actual cost-to-date and the actual EVM-to-date, and take some corrective action. Perhaps he or she would assign

App. B: EVM For Large Projects

different personnel. Maybe the leader would seek input from others. Perhaps, a funding adjustment would be required. The 'leader' may choose to siffon off some of the project reserve to fund this more difficult project, just as a military leader sets aside some of his troop reserves, who can remain fresh, and be applied as needed to critical points in a campaign. The 'reserve' in either case is assigned where it is needed most.

In any case, EVM allows a 'leader' to exercise greater control over a large project. All one has to do is plot the planned EVM for each major WBS element, and to the degree of controllability desired. One can do this down to the smallest WBS element, if so desired. In addition, one can plot the actual EVM on a monthly (or weekly) basis, to see how the project and its sub-elements are performing against expectations (the EVM plan).

The insight and knowledge obtained by such implementation is remarkable. It is yet one more tool that allows a project 'leader' better control over a difficult and large development project. However, the down side is the cost and time required to implement such a measurement system.

The project 'leader' usually decides whether to implement such a plan, by examining the size of the project. By so doing, a judgement can be made as to whether the extra effort, complexity and cost is worth the effort or is productive given the additional cost to do so, especially on large projects.

However, at times, the customer may require implementation of EVM in the contract. In such a case, the cost to implement EVM has already been included in the prior proposal.

We have intentionally not discussed many of the

important technical parameters utilized in the implementation of EVM. Such discussion of BCWS (Budgeted Cost of Work Scheduled) or ACWP (Actual Cost of Work Performed) and others, or of some metrics, such as CV (Cost Variance) and SV (Schedule Variance), or CPI (Cost Performance Index) and SPI (Schedule Performance Index) has not taken place here, in order to keep the discussion fairly non-technical. Nonetheless, parameters such as these, and others are used by the development Project Manager to monitor his or her project's performance in many areas.

Appendix C:

Some Key Contract Types (Not Exhaustive)

Thoughts On Leadership

Appendix C: Some Key Contract Types (Not Exhaustive)

In this Appendix, we will attempt to clarify some (but not all) of the key development and support contract types, used by the U.S. Government. We will try to identify which contract type may be best used for various types of activities. The discussion here will address, LOE, T&M, FFP, CPFF, CPIF and CPAF contract types. Other types are left to the reader to pursue.

LOE: This means Level of Effort. It is usually used for support or maintenance types of activities, which require a relatively low level of risk and for non-development activities. LOE and T & M contracts are often used interchangeably for this type of activity. Usually, no material is required for the LOE type of contract, whereas material charges are allowed under a T & M contract.

T&M: This means Time and Material. It is usually used for low-risk non-developmental activities wherein material and/or labor is applied against the contract. A loaded labor rate and material rate is negotiated with the customer. However, it is rarely used for development type or for high risk type efforts.

The problem can be that the negotiated loaded labor rate may not reflect the actual average loaded labor rate of the implementers assigned to do the work. By loaded, we mean that Overhead and MODC (Material and Other Direct

Costs, such as metal fabrication) rates are applied beyond the unloaded hourly labor rate. If the actual loaded rates do not accurately reflect the negotiated rates, the results can be very positive (negotiated rates> actual average loaded rates) or very negative (negotiated rates< actual average loaded rates). Very negative implies cost overruns. Unless the negotiated rate is greater than the actual average loaded rate, this contract vehicle ought to be avoided in development situations. Sadly, this is not always so.

FFP: This means Firm Fixed Price. it is usually applied to production type contracts, wherein the high risk development has been completed under some kind of Cost Plus contract (CPFF, CPIF or CPAF) and the risk is therefore low. The fee is fixed at so many dollars which represents some fixed fee amount. This is rarely and incorrectly used at times for development activities. If used, it can result in significant losses for the contractor, since there is no reimbursement for costs that exceed the original negotiated amount. In other words, the contractor must assume all cost overrun liability in high-risk development type jobs. Hence, this contract type is generally unsuitable for development projects, but is very suitable for production runs.

CPFF: This means Cost Plus Fixed Fee. This is a cost reimbursable type of contract. In other words the fee is a fixed absolute dollar amount but since the risk in development is usually high, any cost overrun is reimbursed by the customer. However the relative fee diminishes as the cost overrun increases from the original fee amount (in % fee, or in relative terms, but not in terms of absolute fee dollars).

App. C: Some Key Contract Types

CPIF: This is yet another Cost Plus contract type. It means Cost Plus Incentive Fee. It is often used by a customer to incentivize the contractor to meet the financial goals of the project or contract. A financial schedule is usually provided describing what fee will be assigned in meeting certain financial goals.

CPAF: This is one more Cost Plus contract type. It means Cost Plus Award Fee. Again, it is often used by a customer to incentivize the contractor to meet the goals of the project or contract, other than financial, such as schedule. Definition is usually provided in the contract describing what fee type will be awarded in meeting any of these goals.

There is a definite reason for choosing a given contract type, depending upon the level of risk, whether there is to be any cost or risk sharing, production follow through, or support involved.

It is not always possible but sometimes the project manager or the proposal manager may be aware of the potential for large losses, because the contract vehicle is inappropriate for the endeavor being estimated. It is therefore important to examine the contract type that is being requested or proposed. This may seem unimportant. However, I have seen situations where Firm Fixed Price (FFP) projects were requested or proposed for projects that required high-risk development, and the 'expected' overruns did materialize resulting in large financial losses for the company.

I have seen other cases wherein a Time and Material (T&M) contract vehicle was requested or proposed, wherein the pre-negotiated loaded labor rates were lower than the average rate considered to do the required development work. In each case, upper management was made aware of the disconnect and of the very real probability of huge financial losses should the contract be awarded to the contractor.

In each case, the contract was indeed awarded and significant losses did materialize. The lesson: Always examine the contract type for proper applicability, and act accordingly.

Appendix D: General Discussion

Appendix D:
General Discussion

The role of a project 'leader' is to ensure a project's success by the various means available to him or her. The cosmos operates on a principle called 'entropy'. Sounds complicated doesn't it? However, it is really quite straight forward. 'Entropy' is a term used in physics and engineering, meaning 'disorder'. All systems in the cosmos tend to proceed from a state of order to one of greater disorder, and therefore towards one of increased 'entropy'. The same is true of projects. Only the 'leader' can have any hope of preventing this from occurring by utilizing many of the characteristics and tools mentioned in this book.

Written and documented communication is essential. Many huge projects have missed this main point and have suffered huge losses as a result of ignoring or failing to understand this simple, 'common sense' precept.

A 'leader' succeeds by means of being astute, questioning and insightful. Never accept anything at face value, on a project or even in real life. Learn to question every assumption. Never assume that one's staff will 'follow-through' on your vision or your instructions. As President Reagan once said: "Trust but verify". Boy, is that true!

During the American Civil War, Confederate General Hood once created a brilliant plan to stop the Union forces from reaching Franklin, Tennessee. His plan was to be executed near Spring Hill, Tennessee. However, he failed as an effective 'leader'. Why? Because he failed to verify that his junior commanders executed his plan as directed. They did not do so, and therefore, the Union Army reached Franklin and the Confederate Tennessee Army was esentially destroyed. Lulled into a false sense of security, he had falsely assumed that his brilliant plan would be executed as he commanded. These same junior commanders had previously acknowledged Hood's Spring Hill plan and had even concurred with it. The key to success was follow-through. A plan may be brilliant but if it is not properly executed and verified to be so done, then none of it matters, because failure will then result.

A 'leader' needs information constantly, updated at a higher rate for fast changing projects and at a slower rate for slower change projects. What is information? According to Shannon, information is inversely proportional to the probability of knowing something. In other words, if something is already known it contains no information value. However, the less that is known the higher its information content. Information gathering is about learning that which is less known.

In addition, an effective 'leader' uses 'feedback' to correct assumptions and to learn what is actually happening, in real time. This means feedback from the customer and from the staff. It may also mean feedback from the corporate executive staff.

Feedback can be obtained by means of Management By Walking Around (MBWA), and by hosting regular meetings with the customer and with the staff. Otherwise entropy or chaos creeps back in again, and project success becomes less likely.

Effective feedback is also obtained by means of documentation, reviews, specifications, etc. In a Retail environment, feedback is primarily obtained by MBWA and by holding staff meetings. In other words, actual observation can lead to discovery of areas for improvement and necessary change. In that sense, MBWA is a very important observational tool and it should be utilized wherever and whenever possible.

Thoughts On Leadership

About the Author

About The Author: John P. McWilliams, has worked at five different engineering development companies over the past 38 years. He started at a large defense contractor, in Wayland, MA, and continued on to work at several Silicon Valley 'Hi-tech' development companies.

He has designed and managed the development of radar, radar warning and telecommunications equipment. He has obtained a wealth of experience in both the design and the management of development projects for the U. S. and foreign governments.

He has grown from engineer to task manager to project manager, to the positions of Department Manager for Programs & Systems Development to his final position as MSD (Multichannel Systems Division) Director of Programs (projects), at his final place of employment, a high-tech. Silicon Valley company.

As a project manager, he has personally managed more than one dozen projects of all contract types and he was approached numerous times by department managers, program managers and company founders to 'fix' broken (i.e. 'failing') projects. In each case, Mr. McWilliams, together with great technical teams, achieved success and turned problem projects around.

Because of his success at managing many complex, difficult projects, sometimes simultaneously, he became the department manager for Programs & Systems Development at the last company he worked for. Later, in the same company, he was awarded the position of MSD Programs Director, wherein, he was responsible for setting project and design standards, and for overseeing more than 50 projects each month, over four states with a combined revenue of approximately $75 million.

He retired to New Mexico in 2007, where he now writes both fiction and non-fiction books. He has formed two companies: Bria Ventures LLC and Apache Management Consulting LLC (Please see next page for the website).

The first company is related to his non-management writing of fiction, non-fiction, poetry and memoirs of his younger days in Scotland (where he was raised until he was nearly ten years of age) and the Bronx. The second company deals with management consulting and training topics.

He is a member of: National Association of Distinguished Professionals, National Professionals of Excellence and the Institute of Electrical and Electronic Engineers. He is also associated with five historical societies, and numerous writing organizations.

He has published numerous non-fiction and fiction books. He has also written and published several memoirs and books with poetic content. He has also written numerous newspaper and magazine articles, and he has presented six lectures on Apache Warrior Woman, Lozen. He has crafted numerous management/leadership MS Power Point presentations for his management company. This is his first book on the topic of Leadership and Management.

www.ingramcontent.com/pod-product-compliance
Lightning Source LLC
Chambersburg PA
CBHW070241190526
45169CB00001B/260